"A splendid contribution to contemp
a refreshing voice who broadens our
of the worship lives of real people. T
understanding of the relation between
of disciplines can enrich our apprec.

John F. Baldovin, SJ
Professor of Historical and Liturgical Theology
Boston College School of Theology and Ministry

"If the liturgy is the 'summit and source' of church life, as Vatican II asserts, what is the relation between it and daily life? Beside the liturgy celebrated in the church, is there the 'liturgy of life'? If so, what is the relation between these two liturgies? This is no ivory-tower disquisition but a life-and-death issue for Christian life. No one is better equipped to help us understand this connection and live it than Ricky Manalo, who brings his mastery of sociology of religion, ritual studies, liturgiology, popular devotions, spirituality, and cultural studies to bear on this complex issue. His book will be of enormous help not only to theologians and liturgists but also to pastoral ministers, especially bishops and priests."

Peter C. Phan
Ellacuría Chair of Catholic Social Thought
Georgetown University

"This is a timely, important, and stimulating book. Through ethnographic research and a rereading of key texts of the liturgical movement, Ricky Manalo maps a way toward a broadened understanding of liturgy, namely, as encompassing *all* worship practices of the faithful. With this, he contributes to overcoming an older, unhelpful division of worship practices into 'liturgy' on the one hand and so-called paraliturgical practices or popular devotions on the other hand (a division that has plagued liturgical scholarship for far too long). I very much appreciate this approach. More power to books like Ricky Manalo's *The Liturgy of Life*."

Teresa Berger
Professor of Liturgical Studies & Thomas E. Golden Jr.
Professor of Catholic Theology
Yale Divinity School

"In *The Liturgy of Life* Ricky Manalo has moved the discussion about the relationship between the official liturgy of the church and popular expressions of the faith into new and very productive territory. By studying questions about liturgy and the real worship experience of 'the people in the pews' using an interdisciplinary approach employing theology, history, and the social sciences, Fr. Manalo offers new insights that can only benefit pastoral theologians and all those who seek to serve the liturgy."

Mark R. Francis, CSV
President, The Catholic Theological Union

Ricky Manalo, CSP

The Liturgy of Life

The Interrelationship of
Sunday Eucharist and
Everyday Worship Practices

A PUEBLO BOOK

Liturgical Press   Collegeville, Minnesota
www.litpress.org

A Pueblo Book published by Liturgical Press

Cover design by Jodi Hendrickson. Cover image: Dreamstime.

Unless otherwise noted, excerpts from documents of the Second Vatican Council are from *Vatican Council II: The Basic Sixteen Documents*, by Austin Flannery, OP, © 1996 (Costello Publishing Company, Inc.). Used with permission.

1	2	3	4	5	6	7	8	9

Library of Congress Cataloging-in-Publication Data

Manalo, Vincent.
    The liturgy of life : the interrelationship of Sunday eucharist and everyday worship practices / Vincent Manalo, CSP.
        pages   cm
    "A Pueblo book."
    Includes bibliographical references and index.
    ISBN 978-0-8146-6308-0 — ISBN 978-0-8146-6333-2 (ebook)
        1. Spiritual life—Catholic Church.   2. Worship.   3. Lord's Supper—Catholic Church.   4. Catholic Church—Doctrines.   I. Title.

BX2350.3.M2555   2014
264'.02036—dc23

                                                          2014016183

To Mary E. McGann, RSCJ,
in deep appreciation
for your friendship, wisdom, and accompaniment
throughout my doctoral studies;

and to the Community of St. Agnes Church

Contents

Acknowledgments

The writing of this book would not have been accomplished if it were not for the support of many academic colleagues, community members, family, and friends. First and foremost, I wish to thank Mary McGann for being my academic adviser throughout my doctoral studies at the Graduate Theological Union and for serving as coordinator of my dissertation. Her mentoring and friendship remain sources of grace in my life. I also wish to thank Peter Phan for mentoring me along the path of academia. His writings and insights continue to inspire my theological imagination. In addition, I remain grateful to Andrea Bieler, who served as a member of my dissertation committee, and Lizette Larson-Miller, who served as a member of my comprehensive exams committee. I extend my gratitude to the other liturgy professors of GTU, including Michael Aune, John Klentos, Ruth Meyers, Tom Scirghi, and Louis Weil. My interest in liturgical studies took a "sociological turn" when I studied under Ann Swidler of UC Berkeley, and it continued under the guidance of Jerome Baggett of the Jesuit School of Theology. I thank both of these scholars for introducing me to the world of sociology.

I wish to express my appreciation to the members of the parish community of St. Agnes Church, San Francisco, for making me feel welcomed and for allowing me to perform an ethnographic study of their worship practices, and to the parish staff, Rev. Ray Allender, SJ (pastor), Frank Uranich, Scott Grinthal, Zack Zweber, and Frank Mitchell. A heartfelt thanks goes out to my support team at St. Agnes, Rosemary Robinson, Frank Uranich, and Justin Walsh, and the participants of my ethnographic interviews, including Helen Chen Abrams; S. Janet Chau, RSM; David and Rosemarie Dittman; Irene Duller; Mark Durst; Mark Malaspina; Tom Matty; Jude Pendland; Rachel Pinette; James Robinson;

Helen Rosario; Tim Szarnicki; Sally and Gene Tongson; and Edward Williams.

Next, I wish to thank members of my Paulist community for their support, particularly former presidents Frank DeSiano, John Duffy, and Mike McGarry and current president Eric Andrews; my brothers at Old St. Mary's Cathedral in San Francisco; my classmate Brett Hoover, whose passion for pastoral theology kept me grounded in reality; and George Fitzgerald for his friendship and support throughout the writing of this book.

Thanks to the entire staff at Liturgical Press, particularly Peter Dwyer, director; Hans Christoffersen, publisher of the academic department; and Lauren L. Murphy, managing editor. Because this is my first book with the Press, I feel truly honored and humbled! I am also deeply grateful for the friendship and wonderful editorial eye of Denise Anderson, who assisted me during the final stages. You are amazing!

And finally, to my parents, Pat and Dom; my siblings, Lyn, Dom, Riza, Robert, and Chris; and to my dear close friends, Paul, Len, Bob, and Alazar: You are all a blessing to me as you remain forever close to my heart!

Abbreviations

DD	The Lord's Day (*Dies Domini*, 1998)
EE	On the Eucharist in its Relationship to the Church (*Ecclesia de Eucharistia*, 2003)
IL	Liturgical Institutions (*Institutions Liturgiques*, 1841)
LG	Dogmatic Constitution on the Church (*Lumen Gentium*, 1964)
LL	The Liturgical Year (*L'Année Liturgique*, 1841–1875)
MC	On the Holy Eucharist (*Mirae Caritatis*, 1902)
MCC	Mystical Body of Christ (*Mystici Corporis Christi*, 1943)
MD	The Sacred Liturgy (*Mediator Dei*, 1947)
PO	Decree on the Ministry and Life of Priests (*Presbyterorum Ordinis*, 1965)
SC	Constitution on the Sacred Liturgy (*Sacrosanctum Concilium*, 1963)
SOC	The Sacrament of Charity (*Sacramentum Caritatis*, 2007)
STS	On Frequent and Daily Reception of Holy Communion (*Sacra Tridentina Synodus*, 1905)
TLS	The Restoration of Church Music (*Tra le Sollecitudini*, 1903)

Introduction

All Glory Be to Invisible Mary

My earliest memories of praying can be traced back to the daily recitation of the family rosary during my childhood years. We began this devotional practice when I was only six years old. Each and every night my mother would gather her six children together. During that first year she would lead us through the sequence of Hail Marys and Our Fathers. Eventually each of the children would be given the responsibility of leading the rosary, but only after the child had memorized all fifteen "mysteries"[1] and could recite them forward and backward. Memorizing all fifteen mysteries was not the challenge: the challenge was maintaining interest and remaining attentive throughout the prayer. One day my mother thought of a brilliant solution: she suggested that we imagine Mary walking around the room as we recited the rosary. "Our Lady is invisible," she said, "and even though we can't see her, she walks around this room every time we pray the rosary . . . and she's always smiling!" It worked. Every night I imagined an invisible Mary walking around the room, always smiling and always making sure we paid attention. At other times, other saints would join our family, particularly if it was a special feast day, but by and large Mary had

---

[1] The fifteen mysteries of the rosary consist of fifteen events in the lives of Jesus and Mary that are meditated upon during the recitation of this litany. The mysteries are divided into three groups: the *Joyful Mysteries* (the Annunciation, Visitation, Nativity, Presentation, and the Finding of the Child Jesus in the Temple); the *Sorrowful Mysteries* (the Agony in the Garden, the Scourging, the Crowning with Thorns, the Carrying of the Cross, and the Crucifixion); and the *Glorious Mysteries* (the Resurrection, Ascension, Descent of the Holy Spirit, Assumption of the Blessed Virgin Mary into Heaven, and Coronation of the Blessed Virgin Mary as Queen of Heaven).

become my spiritual mother and the primary symbol of holiness. We continued to perform this daily family ritual each night for approximately the next ten years, until my siblings and I eventually moved out of the house and, one by one, went our separate ways. Naturally there were some days when we were unable to pray the rosary together, but those were few and far between.

Two years after we began this practice, during one of my religious education classes, the teacher, Mrs. Brunori, spent part of the class teaching us about devotions to the saints. At one point she opened up a discussion about the rosary, a devotional exercise with which I was well familiar. During that lesson she asked the class: "*To whom* do we pray the rosary?" The answer was obvious to me, and so I raised my hand and answered, "Mary, the Mother of God!" She looked at me but did not respond right away. Instead, she paused, waiting for others to respond, but nobody came forward. Why this pause? I thought to myself. Could I be wrong? After all, why else would "Invisible Mary" walk around our house each night? After a few moments, Mrs. Brunori broke the silence and said, "Well, we pray to Mary . . . but we *really* pray to God." Except for those words I do not recall her exact words in detail, but she somehow explained that, in the end, Mary takes up all of our prayers and presents them to God. I had already *known* this deep inside me (perhaps at one point my mother may have explained this to my siblings and me), but somehow my world was turned upside down at that moment. It was not that my answer was wrong *per se.* After all, we begin those prayers with "Hail Mary." But in hindsight I can see that my image of Invisible Mary had a functional purpose of keeping me attentive (as my Mom told me years later), and the image of Mary walking among us spoke to my heart more than any other theological explanation of her mediating role. I had never seen a picture of God; I didn't know how "He" looked. There was a more intimate connection between Mary and me; Mary, as Mother, was more comforting than God, as Father, and, *deep down inside of me,* she was more real and more personal.

In addition to the family home, the other primary location where my family prayed was in a church building each week at Sunday Mass. But, oddly enough, I do not have any strong memories of "going to Mass" until I was eight years old, two years after we had begun praying the family rosary. My loss of any memory of these weekly events is probably due to the fact that my family moved around a lot during the first six years of my life. Even so, my earliest memory of celebrating was "First Confession" when I was eight years old, at St. Gabriel's Church in Marlboro, New Jersey. For the first time, I stepped into a confessional and proceeded to tell Fr. Sullivan, the associate pastor, my sins, which probably consisted of unkind acts toward my siblings and being irresponsible in performing house chores. Memorizing the opening prayer and the act of contrition was easy: I had become quite skilled in memorizing a litany of prayers that always accompanied the last portion of our daily family rosary. And while I do not remember the penance Fr. Sullivan assigned me, I remember feeling quite relieved when I walked out of the confessional and returned to the pew. What is even more remarkable is that I do not recall the details of my First Holy Communion service, just a couple of months later, save one image: my older sister dressed in a white dress (we celebrated this event together that same year). Beyond that image, not much exists in my memory bank. No doubt First Confession and First Holy Communion were pivotal sacramental events in my childhood. But as it turns out, my fondness for Invisible Mary and praying the rosary with my family each night in our home has become the earliest and most vivid religious memory of my entire life.

An Interaction of Worshipful Practices

The story of my childhood memories of praying the rosary with my family in our home and going to First Confession at St. Gabriel's Church is not meant to suggest that I find no value in Sunday Mass. On the contrary, today I participate more in eucharistic liturgies on average than I pray the rosary. But at the same time, other forms of everyday worship practices have emerged since my childhood, including presiding at daily Mass every Thursday morning at Old St. Mary's Cathedral (the place where I reside); composing liturgical music, often late at night while I am alone in the church and I have the piano all to myself; reciting Morning Prayer and Evening

Prayer from the Breviary with other members of my religious community (or by myself on the iPad); and drinking Japanese tea every day at 4:00 PM on my tatami mat, a time when I either reflect on the scriptural readings of the day, prepare for an upcoming homily I have to deliver, or simply sit in the quietude of God's presence. Becoming aware of and responding to God's presence is my simple definition of worship. In each of the worship practices I mentioned above there is recognition of being in the presence of God, either by myself or with other people, and there is a response to this presence. The responses take different forms, some more explicit than others, and involve different elements. As Dwight W. Vogel suggests in his reflection on "worship," some of these elements may include prayer and praise, lament and thanksgiving, confession and commitment. These elements may be manifested through ritual expressions, but they are not restricted to those expressions. Praise of God is worship whether or not it is embodied in ritual.[2]

While the purposes and goals of each of these worship practices are varied, so too are the locations in which each of them takes place: the side chapel of Old St. Mary's Cathedral for daily Mass, at the piano in the main church to the left of the sanctuary, the rectory chapel, and my Japanese tea room. So are the days of the week and the times of the day: 7:30 AM for daily Mass, 10:00 PM for composing, 8:30 AM for Morning Prayer, 6:00 PM for evening prayer, and 4:00 PM for tea.

Since the start of my doctoral studies at the Graduate Theological Union, I have often reflected on the interactions that exist among the various worship forms people cultivate. These reflections, in turn, led to a conviction that an examination of these interactions could be beneficial to scholars in the field of liturgical studies. For example, the worship practices I listed above not only take place at different locations, on different days of the week, and at different times of the day; they also dynamically interact with one another. During my tea drinking on Wednesday afternoons I usually pre-

[2] Dwight W. Vogel, "Liturgical Theology: A Conceptual Geography," 3–14 in *Primary Sources of Liturgical Theology: A Reader* (Collegeville, MN: Liturgical Press, 2000), at 5.

pare for the homily I will deliver the next day during Thursday daily Mass. The scriptural readings and presidential prayers of Thursday daily Mass, in turn, are usually connected to the previous Sunday Mass, which, in turn, is connected to the larger liturgical season of the church year. At the same time, during other times when I drink tea I make no intentional connections between the quietude of recognizing God's presence and any eucharistic celebration. All of this is to suggest that there is always an interplay between Sunday Eucharist and other worship practices. Sometimes these practices influence each other; at other times they do not.

Considerations of the Cultural Context of Liturgy after the Second Vatican Council

At the time of the Second Vatican Council (1962–1965), the church's self-awareness of its ecclesial identity within the larger global context, coupled with its rich history of Christian missionary activities and the social scientific tools that were made available from anthropological disciplines, contributed to corollary concerns between worship practices and the cultural contexts in which these practices took place. Calling for a revision of the liturgical books, the *Constitution on the Sacred Liturgy* (1963) addressed cultural adaptation of the rites in articles 37–40 and consequently opened the door for "legitimate variations and adaptations" during liturgical celebrations:

> Provisions shall also be made, when revising the liturgical books, for legitimate variations and adaptations to different groups, regions, and peoples, especially in mission lands, provided that the substantial unity of the Roman Rite is preserved; and this should be borne in mind when drawing up the rites and devising rubrics.[3]

The liturgical reforms that emerged out of the Second Vatican Council opened the way for the critical evaluation of the Roman Rite—marked by centuries of European classical form—in light of

---

[3] SC 38.

5

the cultural practices, rituals, symbols, and worldviews of local church contexts. As scholars and pastoral leaders investigated the ecclesial identity and liturgical activities of the church in relation to the rest of the world, "cultural groups" were viewed as being bounded by geographical, national, racial and ethnic realities. More recently, Gerald Arbuckle described this "modern approach to culture" as a type of "billiard ball" model of cultures as separate, impenetrable units, passing with little or no change from one generation to the next in a quasi-automatic way, self-integrating to maintain the status quo, resistant to external influences, homogeneous, and devoid of internal dissent.[4]

Around the same time that the Council convened, a new branch of anthropology, "symbolic anthropology,"[5] was emerging and offering scholars new tools for assessing the cultural dimensions of worship. Works in this field at that period included those of Clifford Geertz,[6] Mary Douglas,[7] and Victor Turner.[8] For example, in Geertz's method of "thick description," interpreters of ritual events observe symbolic actions within which are embedded the worldview, values, and ethos of the particular culture. The symbolic action speaks for itself (the action is the text), but the inter-

[4] Gerald A. Arbuckle, *Culture, Inculturation, and Theologians: A Postmodern Critique* (Collegeville, MN: Liturgical Press, 2010), 4. See also Alan Barnard, *History and Theory in Anthropology* (Cambridge: Cambridge University Press, 2000), 158–84; Kathryn Tanner, *Theories of Culture: A New Agenda for Theology* (Cambridge: Cambridge University Press, 1997), 3–58.

[5] I borrow this term from Sherry B. Ortner, who provides the qualification that "symbolic anthropology" "was never used by any of its main proponents" as a label during its formative years (1963–66), but was "a shorthand tag (probably invented by the opposition), an umbrella for a number of rather diverse trends." See her "Theory in Anthropology Since the Sixties," *Comparative Studies in Society and History* 26 (Jan. 1984): 126–66, at 128.

[6] Clifford Geertz, *The Interpretation of Cultures* (New York: Basic Books, 1973).

[7] Mary Douglas, *Natural Symbols: Explorations in Cosmology* (New York: Pantheon Books, 1982).

[8] Victor Turner, *The Forest of Symbols: Aspects of Ndembu Ritual* (Ithaca, NY: Cornell University Press, 1967); idem, *The Ritual Process: Structure and Anti-Structure* (Chicago: Aldine, 1969); idem, *Dramas, Fields and Metaphors* (Ithaca, NY: Cornell University Press, 1974).

preter (i.e., the voice that speaks "from the actor's point of view") must decipher the various layers of meanings embedded in the presentation. Geertz's hermeneutical approach focuses on the observed event front and center; all other cultural symbols, activities, and representations that surround the event are then placed in alignment with the observable presentation. Geertz's approach to cultural analysis assumed that the observable cultural representation, by way of the anthropologist's interpretation(s), signified the entire way of life of a people and thus fortified the seeming boundaries of cultural identity.[9]

[9] Among the many critiques of Geertz's *The Interpretation of Cultures* (1973), Ann Swidler outlines some of the "causal assumptions" that arise from his method of thick description: "Geertz prefers exploring ritual events that deeply engross their participants. But whatever piece of culture he chooses, his method is the same. He focuses on a cluster of symbols, moving out from that core to the social and symbolic experience within which it has meaning. Thus he 'interprets' the Balinese cockfight by following the many strands of Balinese life that wrap themselves around this vivid public play: Balinese conceptions of animality in human nature, the symbolic sexual significance of cocks, the status rivalries played out in betting on cockfights, and the excitement added to the sport by Indonesian government attempts to outlaw it." See her *Talk of Love: How Culture Matters* (Chicago: University of Chicago Press, 2001), 20. For earlier critiques of Geertz see Talal Asad, "The Construction of Religion as an Anthropological Category," 27–54 in idem, *Genealogies of Religion: Discipline and Reasons for Power in Christianity and Islam* (Baltimore: Johns Hopkins University Press, 1993), first published as "Anthropological Conceptions of Religion: Reflections on Geertz," *Man* 18 (1983): 237–59; Paul Shankman, "The Thick and the Thin: On the Interpretive Theoretical Program of Clifford Geertz," *Current Anthropology* 25 (1984): 261–79; James Clifford and George E. Marcus, eds., *Writing Culture: The Poetics and Politics of Ethnography* (Berkeley: University of California Press, 1986), particularly Vincent Crapanzano's entry, "Hermes' Dilemma," 68–76 in this volume; Mark A. Schneider, *Culture and Enchantment* (Chicago: University of Chicago Press, 1993); Richard Biernacki, "Method and Metaphor after the New Cultural History," 62–92 in *Beyond the Cultural Turn: New Directions in the Study of Society and Culture*, eds. Victoria E. Bonnell and Lynn Hunt (Berkeley: University of California Press, 1999); Stephen Greenblatt, "The Touch of the Real," 14–29 in *The Fate of "Culture": Geertz and Beyond*, ed. Sherry B. Ortner (Berkeley: University of California Press, 1999).

The works of symbolic anthropologists influenced the field of liturgical scholarship in the years after the Council. While this turn to the social sciences does not represent the first time liturgists have "looked over the shoulders of anthropologists," [10] the time period in which these anthropologists wrote coincided with the pastoral implementation of the Second Vatican Council. For example, in her 1975 address during the second annual conference of professional American liturgists, [11] liturgical theologian Mary Collins, a student of Victor Turner, set out "to do cross-disciplinary study of the various anthropological approaches to the study of rite." In her address she urged liturgists to study the rites more holistically by extending the horizon of ritual inquiry beyond textual analysis and by including cross-disciplinary methods that were surfacing in anthropology and ritual studies. [12] In 1991 another liturgical theolo-

---

[10] In his 1989 assessment of the relationship between anthropology and liturgical studies Martin D. Stringer makes note of E. O. James's *Christian Myth and Ritual: A Historical Study* (London: J. Murray, 1933) and the contributions of Anton Baumstark's *Comparative Liturgy* (London: Mowbray, 1958) and Gregory Dix's *The Shape of the Liturgy* (London: Dacre, 1945). The latter two liturgical scholars utilized comparative methodologies borrowed from the social sciences. For his part, Nathan D. Mitchell names Romano Guardini (1885–1968) and Louis Bouyer (1913–2004), who both expressed interest in the "anthropological antecedents" of Christian liturgy. See Mitchell, *Liturgy and the Social Sciences* (Collegeville, MN: Liturgical Press, 1999).

[11] Mary Collins, "Liturgical Methodology and the Cultural Evolution of Worship in the United States," *Worship* 49 (1975): 85–102. This article was later revised in her book, *Worship: Renewal to Practice* (Washington, DC: Pastoral Press, 1987), 73–90. See also her "Ritual Symbols and the Ritual Process: The Work of Victor W. Turner," *Worship* 50 (1976): 336–46.

[12] In *Worship: Renewal to Practice*, 90, Collins wrote: "While we all agree that worship is not simply a matter of words, we continue to manifest a bias of the rational, linear culture which has nurtured us. The verbal code continues to be perceived as the clearest expression of the faith horizon of the church. So, studying texts continues to be perceived as the key to finding meanings in liturgical rites . . . Yet the cultural bias and the greater difficulty of gaining access to and control of non-documentary evidence has maximized the importance of texts and minimized the significance of other data in liturgical studies. The procedural model tended to make the text central and other factors more or less peripheral."

gian, Margaret Mary Kelleher, who was also influenced by Turner's work, provided a detailed description of the communion rite as it was performed within a specific location, "one urban parish in the eastern part of the United States." Attempting "to expand the sources of data on Christian liturgy beyond texts to include the actual performance of rites," she interpreted the ritual meanings of the Eucharist as they were performed within this local worship assembly.[13]

While Collins and Kelleher promoted the use of anthropological tools for the empirical investigation of liturgy, another liturgical theologian, Anscar J. Chupungco, focused on the concerns for inculturation and the application of this theological term in the formation of liturgical rites. Beginning in the mid-1970s, Chupungco developed methods for implementing liturgical inculturation that gave primary consideration to local church contexts and created a dialogue between the worship practices that emerge in those contexts and the cultural predilections of Western Christianity that are often embedded within official rites.[14]

The ecumenical scope of liturgical scholars' use of anthropological tools in order to analyze and interpret the local cultural contexts of worship practices is also worth noting. Throughout the 1970s the World Council of Churches adapted the anthropological term "contexualization" to articulate "the process of updating church structures so that they would keep pace with the changes in the modern world."[15] As a follow-up to these dialogues, the Lutheran World Federation set out to explore for itself the conditions and parameters for the inculturation of its own worship tradition by holding a series of consultation meetings from 1993 to 1996. The

[13] Margaret Mary Kelleher, "The Communion Rite: A Study of Roman Catholic Liturgical Performance," *Journal of Ritual Studies* 5 (1991): 99–122.

[14] Anscar J. Chupungco, "Liturgy and Inculturation," 337–75 in *Handbook for Liturgical Studies* 2 (Collegeville, MN: Liturgical Press, 1998); idem, *What, Then, Is Liturgy: Musings and Memoir* (Collegeville, MN: Liturgical Press, 2010).

[15] Anscar J. Chupungco, "Inculturation of Worship: Forty Years of Progress and Tradition," in *Liturgy in a New Millennium: 2000–2003*, ed. Rhoda Schuler (Valparaiso, IN: Institute of Liturgical Studies, 2006). Available online at http://www.valpo.edu/ils/assets/pdfs/chupungco1.pdf, there at p. 2.

participants at those meetings, including Anita S. Stauffer, Gordon Lathrop, and invited guest Anscar Chupungco, wrestled with terminology, questioning whether they should adapt the terms "contextualization" or "inculturation." They also proceeded, with some caution, to fortify specific boundaries between official liturgical rites and extra-liturgical cultural symbols, while remaining open to their interrelationship. As Chupungco writes:

> Many questions were raised and several left unanswered. I reproduced two salient questions. The first . . . was where to set the boundaries to the incursion of culture in Christian worship. Failure to do this could lead to a situation where violence is done to biblical doctrine in order to accommodate culture. It could also happen that the cultural elements that are integrated in worship overly evoke their cultural provenance and thus divert attention from the Christian rite or worse send an altogether different message to the assembly.
>
> Another scenario would be the mere incorporation of cultural elements into Christian worship without the benefit of integrating them. They could be attractive, perhaps even entertaining, but if they are not integrated with the Christian rite they are no more than decorative appendices or cultural tokens with small role to play in the unfolding of the rite.[16]

In January 1996, during its third international consultation, held in Nairobi, Kenya, the Federation published the *Nairobi Statement on Worship and Culture: Contemporary Challenges and Opportunities*.[17] Continuing the concern over the cultural context of Christian worship, the statement identified four parameters: that worship be contextual, cross-cultural, counter-cultural, and transcultural:

> First, it is transcultural, the same substance for everyone everywhere, beyond culture. Second, it is contextual, varying according to the

---

[16] Chupungco, "Inculturation of Worship," http://www.valpo.edu/ils/assets/pdfs/chupungco1.pdf, 3.

[17] *Nairobi Statement on Worship and Culture: Contemporary Challenges and Opportunities*, available online at http://www.worship.ca/docs/lwf_ns.html.

local situation (both nature and culture). Third, it is counter-cultural, challenging what is contrary to the Gospel in a given culture. Fourth, it is cross-cultural, making possible sharing between different local cultures. In all four dynamics, there are helpful principles which can be identified.[18]

In the more recent work *Christian Worship Worldwide: Expanding Horizons, Deepening Practices*,[19] liturgical scholars from the full spectrum of the ecumenical field, including Charles E. Farhadian, John D. Witvliet, Philip L. Wickeri, Seung Joong Joo, Thomas A. Kane, and C. Michael Hawn, drew on the *Nairobi Statement* in order to consider "the tension between the contextual and the cross-cultural, transcultural, and countercultural" as it occurs in "public worship assemblies" throughout the global church, with studies including Kerala, Latin America, Samoa, South Africa, and South Korea.

While methodological and hermeneutical attention continues to be given to the cultural context of worship practices, what is missing in all of these approaches is an intentional consideration of how non-official worship practices, performed by individuals and/or collective groups, continually interact with Sunday Eucharist within the broader temporal and sociocultural realm of everyday life. The turn to the social sciences that emerged after the Second Vatican Council underscored the importance of cultural context for understanding *what* liturgy is and *how* liturgy is experienced and expressed but, by and large, it paid less attention to how everyday worship practices continually influence and interact with official liturgies and with one another.

In this book I contend that liturgical scholars need to consider the place of non-official worship practices in their reflections on Sunday Eucharist. Further, I would posit that broadening the scope and spectrum of what constitute worshipful practices in the everyday lives of Christians and putting these in dialogue with official

[18] *Nairobi Statement*, 1.3.

[19] *Christian Worship Worldwide: Expanding Horizons, Deepening Practices*, ed. Charles E. Farhadian (Grand Rapids: Eerdmans, 2007).

liturgical rites will render our understanding of the meaning-making that transpires in Christian worship more dense, rich, and textured than is currently the case.

The Source and Summit of Christian Life

In addition to demonstrating the various forms of worship practices that occurred during my childhood, the stories I recounted at the opening of this introduction illustrate how powerful images and metaphors come to be forever embedded in our memories. Some of these images become *fixed*: I do not think I will ever pray the rosary again without imagining and feeling the presence of Invisible Mary in the room. In other cases these religious images and metaphors are collective and shared among a group of people. That the Eucharist is "the source and summit" of Christian life is one such image, and it forms the starting point of this book.

One of the most influential achievements of the modern liturgical movement has been the reassertion of the centrality of the Sunday eucharistic liturgy in the everyday life of Christians. This reassertion culminated doctrinally in the Second Vatican Council's *Constitution on the Sacred Liturgy* (1963), which stated that the "liturgy is the summit toward which the activity of the church is directed . . . [and] the fount [source] from which all her power flows" (article 10). As I will demonstrate later, eventually the term "the liturgy" within this article came to be designated as "the Sunday Eucharist" (as a privileged distinction from other forms of official liturgy, such as the *Liturgy of the Hours*), and the entirety of the article, along with the surrounding articles, eventually became truncated to "the Eucharist is the source and summit of Christian life" in official and academic parlance. But there have always been many variations of this phrase, and in each variation the metaphors "source" (sometimes translated as "font") and "summit" (sometimes translated as "peak") remained constant. I never questioned the meaning of the phrase beyond what I had been taught: to paraphrase, "All roads lead to Sunday Mass and all roads flow away from Sunday Mass."

In 2005, at the start of my doctoral program at the Graduate Theological Union, I read a chapter in a book by Peter C. Phan entitled, "Liturgy of Life as Summit and Source of Eucharistic

Liturgy."[20] In that chapter Phan introduced a term I had not heard before, "the liturgy of life," and he placed this term in relationship to "summit and source." Once I started reading his chapter and learned that the liturgy of life was based on Karl Rahner's "liturgy of the world" (a term I had heard during my studies at the Washington Theological Union), I began to understand more clearly what Phan was proposing. For him the liturgy of life consists of the "universal experiences of God and mystical encounters with God's grace in the midst of everyday life, made possible by God's self-gift embracing the whole human history, always and everywhere."[21] In response to the statement in article 10 of the *Constitution on the Sacred Liturgy*, Phan contends that "the liturgy of life is the summit and source of the church's liturgy and not the other way around."[22] Later he suggests that "the liturgy of life and the liturgy of the church constitute the one worship that humanity renders to God and whose center and supreme fulfillment is Jesus Christ."[23] My earlier (uncritical) conviction that the Eucharist was the source and summit of my life had suddenly changed, or at least became nuanced. Phan's article introduced a new paradigm I had not considered before, and *deep down inside of me* his proposal made sense: the Eucharist is not so much the source and center of my life or the church's life; God is.

The Sociology of Lived Religion

Two years later, in the Fall of 2007, I took a course on the sociology of culture taught by Ann Swidler at the University of California,

[20] Peter C. Phan, "Liturgy of Life as Summit and Source of Eucharistic Liturgy: Church Worship as Symbolization of Liturgy of Life?" 257–78 in idem, *Being Religious Interreligiously: Asian Perspectives on Interfaith Dialogue in Postmodernity* (Maryknoll, NY: Orbis Books, 2004). An earlier version of this article appeared as "Liturgy of Life as the 'Summit and Source' of the Eucharistic Liturgy: Church Worship as Symbolization of the Liturgy of Life?" 5–33 in *Incongruities: Who We Are and How We Pray*, eds. Timothy Fitzgerald and David A. Lysik (Chicago: Liturgy Training Publications, 2000).

[21] Phan, "Liturgy of Life as Summit," 268–69.

[22] Ibid., 265.

[23] Ibid., 272.

Berkeley. I realized that up to that point my approach to cultural studies had been largely shaped by anthropological perspectives, and I began to reflect on how sociological studies might come to influence academic approaches to and experiences of Christian liturgies. That course led to the writing of a paper entitled, "Beyond the Boundaries: Sociology and Liturgy," which I presented to my seminar group during the 2008 gathering of the North American Academy of Liturgy in Savannah, Georgia. The goal of that paper was to initiate dialogue between the fields of liturgical studies and sociology. This was a new turn for liturgical scholarship, since post–Vatican II explorations had focused more on cultural anthropology than on any other social science. It is not surprising that few, if any, liturgical theologians drew upon sociology, since methods for demographic and statistical analysis, which marked sociology during that period, did not provide the cultural interpretive tools liturgical theologians were seeking.

Within the last decade, however, the field of the sociology of lived religion has emerged as a critical and promising contribution to the social science fields and to liturgical scholarship. The sociologists who have led this movement include David D. Hall, Nancy T. Ammerman, Meredith B. McGuire, Giuseppe Giordan, and William H. Swatos. These sociologists and others critique past binary approaches that often pitted "official religion" against "popular religion." "Lived religion"—that is, practices of religiosity and spirituality that occur in everyday life—occupies the middle space between and the inclusive space that surrounds official liturgies and non-official worship practices. Furthermore, sociologists of lived religion often privilege locations outside institutional boundaries as starting points of inquiry, and they also remain open to how individuals and collective social groups perform these practices within and around such boundaries.

Outline of the Book

All of these experiences provide the backdrop for and shape the methodological and interpretive tools I will use in this book. My goal is to expand the contextual horizon of liturgical scholarship and to include a broader range of worship practices as appropriate subject matter for our inquiry. After providing some background to my ethnographic project, I will explore a historical evolution of understandings of the phrase "source and summit" as descriptive of the relationship between the Eucharist and all other non-official worship practices. Specifically, I will demonstrate that in the latter part of the twentieth century a notion of the liturgy, particularly the Eucharist, as source and summit vis-à-vis other spiritual religious practices became solidified and was promoted in Roman Catholic teaching. My choice to focus on the Eucharist does not imply that this is the only tradition of liturgical worship that historically has been a part of the church. But for the scope of this book I opted to focus on the Eucharist as representative of official liturgy, as it remains our most formal and central worship practice.

Then I will entertain Peter Phan's revision of "source and summit" as a theological paradigm that includes both Eucharist and other non-official worship practices, all of which constitute the one worship that humanity renders to God. With this theological perspective as a basis, I will introduce the perspectives and methods of sociologists of religion as well as correlations of ethnographic data based on my own exploration of one community's perception of these relationships. It is my contention throughout that examining the dynamic interrelationship between Sunday Eucharist and other forms of worshipful practice that occur in everyday life will reveal new theological, ecclesiological, and ritual understandings of "liturgy" that expand and inform the contextual horizon of liturgical scholarship.

Chapter 1 presents a general introduction to one Roman Catholic worship community in San Francisco, St. Agnes Church, followed by brief background introductions to the participants in my ethnographic project. From February 2010 to June 2012 I was engaged in participant observation of their 10:30 AM Sunday Mass, which took place within their church building, the official worship site of this parish. I also conducted targeted interviews with eight members of this community ("ethnographic participants"), gained deeper insights, and learned of their interpretations of the interrelatedness of the various worship practices in which they engaged. At the beginning of each chapter I will share some of the stories and interpretations that emerged from these interviews.

Chapters 2 and 3 provide the historical background and development of the statement "the Eucharist is the source and summit of Christian life," and demonstrate that articulations of this statement were indicative of the larger goal to identify the relationship between official liturgy and popular religious practices. Chapter 2 will trace the various usages of the term "source and summit" in the official documents and writings of some of the pioneers of the liturgical movement leading up to the Second Vatican Council (roughly 1833–1962). I will provide a brief description of the state of the relationship between the Eucharist and popular religion at the beginning of the movement, thus setting the backdrop for the documents and writings that will follow. Then I will provide brief summaries of how some of the pioneers of this movement came to use the terms "source and summit" in their writings, specifically Dom Prosper Gueranger, Popes Leo XIII and Pius X, Dom Lambert Beauduin, Virgil Michel, and Pius XII. Throughout the entire liturgical movement these ecclesial leaders and liturgical scholars experimented with images such as "source and summit" in order to promote a new fervor that could generate more lay participation during the Eucharist. Unfortunately, the vigorous promotion of the Eucharist eventually led to a decreased emphasis on popular religious practices by the time of the Second Vatican Council.

Chapter 3 focuses on how the image of "the Eucharist as source and summit" came to be articulated in three important documents from the Second Vatican Council and in some of the post-conciliar documents by Popes John Paul II and Benedict XVI. When Vatican II brought together all the energy and fervor of the liturgical movement, the image of the Eucharist as source and summit became even more solidified as the church vigorously promoted its official worship in relation to the rest of Christian life, including all those practices that were deemed devotional, spiritual, or pietistic. I will demonstrate this through several council documents: the *Constitution on the Sacred Liturgy* (1963), the *Dogmatic Constitution on the Church* (1965), and the *Decree on the Ministry and Life of Priests* (1965). This will be followed by an examination of post-conciliar documents, including Pope John Paul II's *The Day of the Lord* (1998) and *On the Eucharist in Its Relationship to the Church* (2003), and Pope Benedict XVI's *The Sacrament of Charity* (2007). In short, all the writings that will be investigated in chapters 2 and 3 will demonstrate that the various articulations of this phrase were indicative of a larger unfolding process that attempted to define and order the interrelationship between official liturgy and non-official worship practices and to place the Eucharist at the top of the worship pyramid. Throughout this process of reordering, the fluidity of interactions between official liturgy and non-official worship practices remained.

Chapter 4 presents in more detail Peter Phan's proposal that the liturgy of life is the source and summit of the Eucharist and popular religion and, further, that both of these worship practices together constitute the one worship that humanity renders to God. Phan offers a theological paradigm that does not limit "worship" to eucharistic liturgies alone but instead broadens the scope and spectrum of what constitutes "liturgy." In doing so he expands the contextual horizon of liturgical scholarship to include a range of personal/communal practices. But where Phan focuses on popular religion as an example of non-official liturgy, this book will consider *all* forms of non-official worship practices as legitimate expressions of Christian faith that could potentially be placed in dialectical relationship with Sunday Eucharist. How I come to approach and understand what is entailed in this spectrum of worship practices will largely depend upon the next two chapters, 5 and 6.

Moving from theological foundation to social scientific methods of investigation, chapter 5 will provide an analysis of the writings of sociologists of lived religion in order to explore the disciplinary methods these sociologists use in their attempts to uncover the pluriform practices of worship that occur in everyday life.[24]

---

[24] The specific writings include David D. Hall's edited volume, *Lived Religion in America: Toward a History of Practice* (Princeton, NJ: Princeton University Press, 1997), Nancy T. Ammerman's *Everyday Religion: Observing Modern Religious Lives* (Oxford and New York: Oxford University Press, 2007), Meredith B.

The works of these sociologists provide one of the methodological foundations for chapter 6, which provides correlations of my ethnographic data. My approach to ethnography is based on the methodologies of Mary E. McGann, who has been at the forefront of applying ethnographic research tools to liturgical studies ("liturgical ethnography"), and of anthropologist James Clifford, who opened up the boundaries of ethnographic field sites by considering the complexities and the "pervasive spectrum of human experiences" that transpire between a variety of locations.

Finally, in chapter 7, I engage in an interdisciplinary conversation among the three perspectives of my study (theological, sociological, and ethnographic), seeking to discover how the data I glean from sociologists of religion and my ethnographic research confirm, stretch, and recontextualize the theological framework I have drawn from Peter Phan regarding the liturgy of life. I will end with a presentation of how my work contributes to one current issue in the field of liturgical studies: the centrality of divine initiative in liturgical worship, and hence in liturgical-theological reflection.

McGuire's *Lived Religion: Faith and Practice in Everyday Life* (Oxford and New York: Oxford University Press, 2008), and Giuseppe Giordan and William H. Swatos's edited volume, *Religion, Spirituality and Everyday Practice* (Dordrecht and New York: Springer, 2011).

Chapter One

Welcome to St. Agnes!

Jude Penlands's eyes beam with excitement when I ask her why she goes to St. Agnes Church for the Sunday Eucharist. She shares a story about a conversation she had with a friend who owns a tourist business, "The Mexican Bus," a city tour guide that takes place within a bus decorated with Mexican emblems and symbols. When her friend asked if she would like to rent the bus and if Jude could find "people to fill it," Jude right away thought of St. Agnes. "Immediately I said, 'Oh God, all I have to do is spread the word in St. Agnes!' *It's like I have a home base there!*"

❖   ❖   ❖

When Helen Chen Abrams moved to her first condominium in the Haight-Ashbury neighborhood (she is a teacher), she started going to St. Agnes and found the preaching and ministries at the parish comparable to those at the Newman Center at the University of California, Berkeley, particularly the openness to gay and lesbian ministries that both parishes promote.

> I started coming here and I *really* like St. Agnes. There was a series of coincidences when [one day] they announced that they're training altar servers and readers. So that's how I started getting involved here, because it was just like . . . I didn't just want to "go to Mass": I wanted to, you know, *do something and help.*

For Helen, "doing something" is her form of everyday worship. She continues: "The way I worship is not necessarily *true* prayer, but more through *service*. I find I try to anchor my week's activities on the teachings of the Gospels. . . . That's why I really like going to church!"

❖   ❖   ❖

In the late afternoon of February 17, 2010, around 5:10 PM, I walked into St. Agnes Church to participate in and observe their 5:30 PM service of Ash Wednesday, the beginning of the Lenten season. The parish is located in the Haight-Ashbury neighborhood of San Francisco.[1] As I walked through the small, narrow, and dark narthex (foyer), I entered the central nave of the church and came upon an open and wide area that took up a full quarter of the entire nave.[2] Nearly twenty years ago the last ten rows of pews had been removed in order to form "the hospitality area," the term used by the pastoral staff to refer to this area.[3] The term "hospitality" mainly refers to the hospitality and social interaction that start *after* Mass ends when, for approximately fifteen to twenty minutes, 50 to 70 percent of the assembly walk over, and, while eating donuts, cookies, cut-up pastries, and drinking coffee, milk, and juice, socialize with one another: "gather with everyone after Mass," "catch up with my friends," "my time to say 'hello' to Fr. Ray Allender [the pastor]," "talk about the homily, whether we liked it or not," "tell Frank [the director of music and liturgy] how much we enjoyed his music," "eat donuts and feel guilty afterwards," and so on. Six of the eight participants I interviewed for this book, when asked why they go to St. Agnes, referred to this "time to catch up with one another." For example, for Rachel Durst, "this is the 'greeting space,' because we are a community of welcome and hospitality." For Edward Williams it was the sense of hospitality he experienced in this space that convinced him to join the parish and become Roman Catholic:

[1] See appendix 1, p. 177.

[2] See appendix 2, p. 179.

[3] At the end of the communion rite of Sunday Eucharist and during the announcements, the cantor, Scott Grinthal, always invites the assembly: "Join us for light refreshments in our hospitality area in the back of the church!"

I came here and the first person I met was Felina. She's very warm. . . . So I met her and then I turned to Frank [the liturgy director]. He told me that the Rite of Christian initiation doesn't start until September. So I met more and more and more people—pretty much I came every week—and they take your photograph and put it on a board [in the hospitality area]. People are coming up to me and saying hi . . . hi . . . hi . . .!

When I was selecting a worship community for this book, this particular space appealed to me at both an inspirational and a practical level. For me the hospitality area represents a *communal* liminal space between official space and the outside world where everyday religious practices occur. It is in the hospitality area that a more intentional communal gathering of ritual transitioning occurs, from the outside world to the inside and vice versa. This is the building's "contact zone," the borderland, where worshipers negotiate the overlapping meanings of worship through social conversation, liturgical preparation, and/or liturgical reflection on the Mass they have just experienced. Since the majority of parishioners "transitioned" into and away from this space, it became the primary (but not the only) place where I conducted casual interviews with the parishioners and the parish staff, before and after the Mass. Thus this space becomes an appropriate image to introduce the readers to the 10:30 AM Sunday Eucharist of St. Agnes Church.

Hospitality, Music Making, and Preaching

The 10:30 AM Masses at St. Agnes Church are well planned, prepared, and performed by all liturgical ministers and the assembly. Based on my interviews with dozens of parishioners over the course of my project, I concluded that the three most common reasons why people choose to worship at St. Agnes are hospitality, music making, and preaching.

Hospitality

There is a vibrant energy level that begins as early as twenty minutes before the start of the Mass, as the assembly members and liturgical ministers converse with one another. This occurs throughout the entire worship space, along the center and two main side aisles, within the pews, near the choir section to the right of the sanctuary (while the choir rehearses) and, of course, in and around the hospitality area. For Rachel Durst, greeting one another at St. Agnes is a prophetic calling. "If we greet one another, we meet the stranger. We let them know that this is the place where all are welcomed." For Helen Chen Abrams, "The people, they're just so nice . . . just *genuinely* nice and I think that's what Christ wanted: to just be nice to each other." By 10:20 AM the noise level throughout the worship space is noticeably heightened with socializing. The start of Mass is ritually timed and planned to begin the moment Scott, the cantor, steps up to the microphone to the right of the sanctuary and announces: "Good morning, everyone! Welcome to St. Agnes!" After a moment's pause he continues, "We invite you to stand and greet others around you." For the next twenty to thirty seconds we turn to those around us, with extended hand reached out for a handshake, or a hug, or a simple gesture of greeting to those across the aisle.

During the Fall of 2009, while I was searching for parishes in the San Francisco Bay area, I surfed the Internet and came across the St. Agnes web page. The home page prominently placed three distinct words that served as a slogan for the parish: Inclusive, Diverse, Jesuit. A more descriptive mission statement followed:

> Saint Agnes Parish is a 117-year-old Roman Catholic Jesuit parish community in the historic and socially conscious Haight-Ashbury district of San Francisco, California. Known for prayerful liturgies, well-prepared homilies, gracious hospitality, and vitality, Saint Agnes Parish draws men and women, young and old, straight and gay from the neighborhood and around the City and beyond to what some call "the last chance church!" It is truly Catholic—all are welcome.[4]

This statement, along with my recognition that this was a Jesuit parish, prompted me to visit.

---

[4] http://www.saintagnessf.com. The parish was founded in 1893. The web page has since been updated.

St. Agnes is a community where those who often feel alienated from the church find themselves welcomed. As Fr. Ray explained:

> It's mostly a white Caucasian parish. Our largest ethnic group, outside of the white population, is the Filipino group. It's also attractive to the gay and lesbian community; they're accepted here and they like a more integrated parish than, say, Most Holy Redeemer in the Castro [neighborhood]. It attracts a lot of people who are disaffected, young people who are looking for something. . . . It's a warm community, and you usually get a good homily. So all of these things come together and make this an attractive place!

The majority of the worshipers during the 10:30 AM Mass are of European American heritage and middle-income. Of the 260 worshipers (the average number according to parish "attendance records" for October 2010 and October 2011), I have noted that at any given Sunday service there is an average of fifteen Africans/African Americans, thirty-three Asian Pacific (mostly Filipino), and fifteen Hispanics/Latinos. Thus nearly 24 percent of the worshipers are non-white. The average breakdown of gender is 138 females and 97 males. There are about twenty-five infants and children below the age of twelve. During the Liturgy of the Word, some twelve to fifteen of these children process out from the pews to the side rooms where they have their own scriptural study, and return to the larger assembly during the preparation of gifts at the beginning of the second half of the Mass.

When I opened the bulletin the first time, I quickly noted a variety of ministerial groups, including Consolation Ministry, Food Pantry, Filipino Community, Legion of Mary Group, Liturgical Ministries, Gay and Lesbian Ministry, Rite for Christian Initiation of Adults (RCIA), Welcoming Ministry, and Young Adult Group. According to the leaders of most of these groups, members of their groups are present for the 10:30 AM Mass and are active in a variety of liturgical roles. Further, the majority of these groups hold, on average, meetings every four to six weeks, with some meetings occurring after the 10:30 AM Mass. As a further testament to this parish's hospitality, lectors are instructed to use inclusive language and women take a prominent leadership and liturgical role. In short, groups who may feel alienated from the Roman Catholic Church or from the larger community of St. Agnes are made to feel welcomed.

Music Making

The assembly participates fully and actively in the singing and playing of music throughout the liturgy. This accomplishment is due in large part to Frank Uranich, who has been a member of this community since 1997.[5] Every Sunday the choir begins to practice around 10:00 AM, in addition to their weekly practice every Tuesday night from 7:30 to 9:00 PM. On average there are twenty members of the choir (five per section: soprano, alto, tenor, and bass), with four paid section leaders. In addition to the piano and organ, which are played by Frank, there is usually a violinist and a cellist. On more solemn occasions such as Christmas Day, Easter Sunday, and Pentecost, there is a brass quartet and a timpanist. Scott, who also serves as the parish secretary, has served as cantor for this Mass for the past fifteen years. While the majority of song selections in the parish music repertoire include the music of contemporary composers, such as Bob Hurd, David Haas, and Dan Schutte, traditional Catholic hymns are also sung.

For some parishioners who worship during this Mass, "the music is the best part of coming to St. Agnes." "You're not gonna get anybody better than Frank!" Fr. Ray exclaimed. Others noted that the choir is "well-rehearsed" and "the time they [the choir] put into practicing their [vocal] parts shows!" Another has commented on "the joyful presence" of Scott whenever he leads the assembly. I always see many of the members of the assembly singing, but noted that more people toward the front half of the pews engage in sung participation. At the end of every Sunday Mass the presiding priest always recognizes the efforts of Frank, Scott, and the entire choir, after which the assembly joins in with enthusiastic applause.

---

[5] Frank states: "I plan all of the liturgies, write the scripts for the presider, general intercessions. I copy them and provide a script to each presider. I make copies of general intercessions and place them in the church, set the ribbons for the Roman Missal. I choose the Preface and the Eucharistic Prayers and plan all of the music and make a weekly worship aid."

This is followed by a listing and acknowledgment of *all* liturgical ministries, including readers, altar servers, eucharistic and hospitality ministers.

Preaching

The content and message of the homily are usually engaging. Each of the three Jesuits who preaches has his own style.[6] On average, homilies last close to ten minutes. Some worshipers described the homilies as "thought-provoking," "spiritual," and "not too long," while many shared their preference of preachers, noting that at times the homilies may be "too heady," "boring," or "repetitive." But as Rachel explains: "I need homilies that are thoughtful, homilies that will allow me to spend some time thinking about one line. It doesn't have to be the whole thing but something that would catch my attention, that will make me say, 'A-ha! I have to remember this in my life!'"

In my own observation the most common themes center on social justice, Christian spirituality, and discernment. The preachers often reference the scriptural readings of the day (primarily the Gospel reading) and interrelate these readings with social responsibility and acts of charity. It is not uncommon for all three preachers to make reference to the Jesuit community, charism, and spirituality.

Meet the Participants of My Ethnographic Project

In selecting a parish community as a base for my ethnographic research project I sought one whose administrative staff would be supportive of my goals and available throughout the course of the project. A supportive and available staff would assist in gathering informational resources (such as access to data concerning demographics) and provide and maintain a network of contacts among parishioners, liturgical leaders, and parish interest groups. Since

---

[6] Besides Ray Allender, the pastor of St. Agnes, the other two Jesuit priests who are part of the preaching and presiding rotation schedule are Frank Buckley and Radmar Jao.

the start of my project the entire staff has been quite supportive of my ethnographic project. They allowed me to include a bulletin insert that detailed my project for the parishioners; they introduced me to the worship community at the end of one Sunday eucharistic liturgy and continually "checked in" with me each week to inquire about my progress.

During the early stage of my project I formed a support team made up of Frank Uranich; Rosemary Robinson, the director of the spiritual life center; and Justin Walsh, the director of the young adult group. I maintained regular contact with my team members throughout the duration of the project.[7] Together we went through a process of discernment that eventually led to the selection of eight participants representing a cross-section of sociocultural backgrounds. I am deeply grateful that they all expressed a high degree of enthusiasm and interest in the project.

Helen M. Rosario

Helen, a widowed Filipina of eighty-seven, has the honor of having been a member of St. Agnes Church longer than any other parishioner. She had been coming to this church since 1954, when she was twenty-nine. She and her husband (twenty years older than she, he has since died) tried for five years to have children. "That [St. Agnes] is where I prayed and prayed to the Sacred Heart to become pregnant . . . and then I become pregnant! That's why I named [my daughter] Agnes!"

[7] During the first six months of my project I met with each of them separately and went over the proposal and goals of the project. During the course of meeting as a group we went through three stages to decide who among the worshipers at the 10:30 AM Mass would best serve as participants for my study, persons with whom I would engage in a series of more targeted interviews about the interrelationship between Sunday Eucharist and everyday worship practices.

Edward Williams

I met Edward[8] at the spiritual life center, an adjacent building to the church building that primarily serves as the parish social center for meetings, workshops, and adult spiritual formation. Edward shared his story of how he found his "higher power" at the age of thirty-four when he attended a service at the Glide Memorial United Methodist Church in the Tenderloin district of San Francisco. He had been dependent on alcohol for many years and decided to join AA. After being raised Baptist (from the age of ten) and continually being told that he "was doomed," he experimented with other denominations, including Pentecostal churches, until he discovered Glide. He found "satisfaction with AA" and eventually "wanted nothing to do with religion." He also felt that "God had abandoned Black people," and he discovered AA at a time when he wanted to "grow spiritually . . . needing something more." His regular attendance at AA meetings led to his encounter with a Jesuit priest who recommended that he visit St. Agnes. He had been searching for "some kind of community . . . something bigger." In his first visit to St. Agnes he was struck by the hospitality of the parishioners and eventually joined the RCIA. Today this seventy-five-year-old African American regularly goes to the 10:30 AM Mass, where he serves as an acolyte and eucharistic minister.

Jude Penland

Jude is a fifty-four-year-old woman, a physical therapist for the San Francisco Giants baseball team. When she is not playing therapist to the Giants she works at St. Francis Hospital. She is happily partnered with a Japanese woman who is Buddhist. She had been trying to "regain her spiritual life" after having been "away from church for many years." She was

---

[8] This name has been changed to protect the subject's identity.

raised as a "high church Episcopalian," but after experiencing a period of "spiritual dryness" in her life she surfed the Internet one day, discovered St. Agnes parish, and joined the community. Two years ago, after searching for a community of religious women to join as a lay person, Jude became an oblate of the Benedictine community of Our Lady of the Rock in Shaw Island, Washington. She visits the monastery about two to three times a year.

Rachel Pinette and Mark Durst

On September 25, 2008, the people of Christ the Light parish in downtown Oakland, California, moved into their newly built cathedral building. After close to twenty years without a cathedral building to call home (their last building was destroyed in the 1989 earthquake), many Catholics of the Diocese of Oakland marked this monumental event as a sign of hope and fulfillment of their prayers. But in the months to follow, not all of the parishioners of Christ the Light remained. For Mark, "the cathedral started to fall apart as a place to get good liturgy. . . . The people who were giving the homilies, the people who were doing the readings, the careful attention to how to do inter-ethnic Masses . . . that was sort of falling apart too." Close to a year and a half later Mark and Rachel began searching for a new parish. They decided to go to St. Agnes, even though they would have to travel across the Bay Bridge and drive thirty minutes each way every Sunday. They have been married for thirty years and have two daughters and a son. Mark is a mathematician and Rachel teaches religion at Bishop O'Dowd High School in Oakland.

Irene Duller and James Robinson

Irene, thirty-five years old, and James, thirty-two years old, are newlyweds. Since the conclusion of my project, Irene has given birth to their first child, Ohio. They were married in St. Agnes Church on November 11, 2011. Irene was brought up by a "God-fearing

Catholic Mom" and was taught "a black-and-white" picture of the world. But she never related to any of this and became "the rebel of the family." She explains: "I think I had an *idea* of God growing up, because I didn't hate God; I just didn't understand the way my parents expressed God in the house." Both Irene and James go to St. Agnes, on

average, once every three months. "I don't think we are less Catholic if we don't go," explains Irene. "Here's the other thing," James chimes in, "after I go I kind of feel like I'm reset . . . reset as a clean slate. I mean obviously I don't pray every day, every night . . . like, thank you for *this* and thank you for *that*, and take care of *this person*, etc. But I make sure to do that in church."

Helen Chen Abrams

Born in Hong Kong, Helen is twenty-eight years old and has been married to a Jewish man, Jacob, for three years. She became a baptized Catholic when she was eight years old, due to her mother's influence (her father is not Catholic). However, before she could receive Confirmation she and her par-

ents moved to Los Angeles and for a few years she stopped going to Mass with her mother since they were not able to find a Chinese Catholic community they liked. One day, while she was studying at the University of California, Berkeley, her classmate invited her to Mass at the Newman Center. She enjoyed the preaching and the social justice ministries at Newman and was eventually confirmed. Today she commutes to St. Agnes Church from San Mateo most

Sundays. "I would put *Sacred Space* [a Lenten prayer booklet] in my iPhone and do prayer during my thirty-minute ride." More recently Helen has given birth to their first child, Quincy.

Unfolding Ethnographic Threads

At the beginning of each of the chapters of this book (as demonstrated above), I will provide brief narrative threads and insights that emerged from my ethnographic project. These threads will eventually be summarized and correlated in chapter 6. But first, due to my desire to use "source and summit" as a starting metaphor of how official church teachings and liturgical theologians came to interrelate the Eucharist with other forms of everyday worship practices, in the next two chapters I will offer a history of how these terms had been used throughout the liturgical movement and in the documents of the Second Vatican Council.

Chapter Two

The Interrelationship between the Eucharist as Source and Summit and Popular Religious Practices during the Liturgical Movement

I believe that the Mass is honoring God, first of all, and then, also, to ask forgiveness of my sins. That's how I feel! And I know that the priest guides us, like the readings of the gospel. I don't have all the time to search for the gospel, but in the Mass he reminds [me] what is the theme for today. So I love to go to Mass. I believe that there's spirituality.

Helen Rosario

I don't know . . . I just feel like I've gotten closer to God. I started thinking about service, ministering to others in whatever ways I can, based on the gifts God has given us. God has given us each different gifts and it's our job to use the gifts that God gave us. So I guess my way of worshiping is to be what Jesus would want us to be. And how Mass fits into that, it's like, you know, you get distracted and worried. I'm getting really stressed out with my [job]. So coming to Mass, it's like a nice reset, like a nice anchor. It's reflection, reflection on parts about my week, and sometimes the readings speak to that. And then, asking myself, what can I do, what can I do?

Helen Chen Abrams

❖   ❖   ❖

The liturgical movement that began in Europe during the nineteenth century has had a lasting impact on Christian worship. One of its many goals was to address the interrelationship between liturgy and Christian life. As André Haquin writes:

> The Liturgical Movement refers essentially to pastoral initiatives and efforts undertaken by groups and individuals to rediscover the meaning of the Church and the liturgy, and the place of the liturgy in the Christian life, in order to encourage "the active participation" of all the baptized and improve the quality of the celebrations; for liturgy is neither the monopoly of the clergy nor a private matter but the celebration of the whole Church.[1]

One of the more prominent images that has been used to describe this relationship is that of the Eucharist as the source and summit of Christian life. During the Liturgical Movement variations of this oft-cited phrase began to emerge, with each variation using some combination of the terms "source" and/or "summit."[2]

Nearly four hundred years later, during the Second Vatican Council, article 10 of the *Constitution on the Sacred Liturgy* (1963) stated: "the liturgy is the summit toward which the activity of the

---

[1] André Haquin, "The Liturgical Movement and Catholic Ritual Revision," 696–720 in *The Oxford History of Christian Worship*, eds. Geoffrey Wainwright and Karen B. Westerfield Tucker (Cambridge: Cambridge University Press, 2006), at 696.

[2] Even before the movement began, the description of the Eucharist as a source existed. For example, this image could be found in the *Catechism of the Council of Trent* (1566): "As however no language can convey an adequate idea of its utility and fruits, pastors must be content to treat of one or two points, in order to show what an abundance and profusion of all goods are contained in those sacred mysteries. This he will in some degree accomplish, if, having explained the efficacy and nature of all the sacraments, *he compare the Eucharist to a fountain*, the other sacraments to rivulets [small streams]. For the holy Eucharist is truly and necessarily to be called the fountain of all graces, containing, as it does, after an admirable manner, the fountain itself of celestial gifts and graces, and the author of all the sacraments, Christ our Lord, from whom, *as from its source*, it is derived. Hence therefore may we easily infer, what most ample gifts of divine grace are bestowed on us by this sacrament." In *The Catechism of the Council of Trent for Parish Priests* (1566) Part II, Chapter IV, Question 45. (Emphasis added.) English translation by Theodore Alois Buckley in *The Catechism of the Council of Trent* (London: Routledge, 1852), 237.

Church is directed" and "the source from which all her power flows." The following year, article 11 of the *Dogmatic Constitution on the Church* (1964) reasserted this relationship, but further specified "the eucharistic sacrifice" as "the source and summit of the whole Christian life." That the Eucharist as "source and summit" remains a popular image for describing the relationship between liturgy and Christian life is demonstrated in the more recent assessment of the *Constitution on the Sacred Liturgy* by Rita Ferrone. Ferrone posits the theological concept of "Liturgy as the 'Summit and Source' of the Church's Life" as one of seven essential concepts of the document, stating that "[t]he place of the liturgy in the life of the Church was a topic of great interest to those who wrote the constitution. A correct understanding of the relationship between liturgy and Church was not something that could be taken for granted; it needed to be stated."[3] Thus at the heart of these uses of the terms "source" and "summit" in describing the liturgy is an attempt to articulate the interrelationship between the official liturgy, especially the Eucharist, and all other Christian activities that mark the everyday life of the church.

In this chapter I will outline a historical overview of how some of the ecclesial leaders and liturgical scholars of the liturgical movement came to understand and articulate the relationship between liturgy and Christian life through their articulation of the Eucharist as source and summit, and how this image came to be interrelated with non-official worship practices, particularly popular religion. First I will briefly describe the context in France with regard to the relationship between eucharistic practices and practices of popular devotions within the larger European landscape. I begin in France since it is generally considered the country where the movement began. Then, in chronological order, I will provide brief summaries of the work of six pioneers of the

---

[3] Rita Ferrone, *Liturgy: Sacrosanctum Concilium* (Mahwah, NJ: Paulist Press, 2007), 25. The other six essential concepts include: the paschal mystery; full, active, and conscious participation; ecclesiology; inculturation; renewal of the liturgical books; music, art, and artifacts of the liturgy; and education and formation. See ibid., 19–50.

movement: Dom Prosper Guéranger, Popes Leo XIII and Pius X, Dom Lambert Beauduin, Virgil Michel, and Pope Pius XII. These men sought to address pastoral concerns because of their conviction that a liturgical renewal would lead to a spiritual renewal among the laity in daily life. I will demonstrate how concern over the relationship between liturgy and popular religion had been a primary one since the start of the movement. However, as the movement progressed, the writings revealed a privileging of the Eucharist by a hierarchical reordering of all other worship practices beneath it.

Setting the Historical Context for the Relationship between the Eucharist and Popular Religion at the Start of the Liturgical Movement

Since there is no single consensus on the beginning date of the liturgical movement, it is better to view it as a progression of interrelated historical strands and sub-movements with roots in nineteenth-century Europe.[4] According to Edward Muir, the liturgical reforms that had emerged from the Council of Trent had developed into two distinct tendencies: "one, regulations imposed from above and the other, pietistic practices expressing lay enthusiasm for Christian renewal."[5] The new liturgical regulations were left to the local bishops, thus leading to a varied, if not uneven, implementation process throughout Europe and the Americas. In France, for example, where the movement is generally known to have started, the dioceses were marked by diverse liturgical prac-

[4] Various theologians and historians have positioned the starting point of this movement at different times and geographical locations. Haquin writes: "Should one speak of a single liturgical movement or rather of several in the modern period? There may be a risk in speaking of a single movement in the case of a multiform action spread out over a century (1833–1963) and freely developed in different countries. It is only after the event that historians, struck by the many convergences and connections, sketch a history of 'the' Liturgical Movement." "The Liturgical Movement and Catholic Ritual Revision," 696–97.

[5] Edward Muir, *Ritual in Early Modern Europe*, 2d ed. (Cambridge: Cambridge University Press, 2005), 224.

tices and popular devotions. Conservative reactions to Gallicanism and Jansenism led to a variety of local attempts to implement the revised Roman Missal of 1570. Yet despite these attempts, full implementation of a uniform eucharistic liturgy was not achieved in France as a whole until 1875.[6]

If eucharistic liturgies remained diverse during the nineteenth century, the various forms of popular religious practices were even more so. Muir suggests that their roots can be traced back to late medieval ritual practices. After the Council of Trent there was a more rapid development of ritual practices among Catholics, "reinvigorated and redeployed" by the laity and clergy, "in part as a Catholic response to the Protestant threat and in part as a general revival of Catholic piety that coincided with the Reformation but was not entirely dependent on it.[7] Mark R. Francis describes this period during the nineteenth century as a Romanization of European devotionalism, since it was marked by a vigorous centralization and control by the Catholic hierarchy of all forms of piety.[8] Similarly to Muir's observation, Francis lists two types of piety that coexisted with one another: "the popular and the official."[9]

---

[6] See Cuthbert Johnson, *Prosper Guéranger (1805–1875): A Liturgical Theologian* (Rome: Pontifical Institute of St. Anselm, 1984), 147–243.

[7] Muir writes: "At every point where Protestant reformers had criticized traditional ritual practices—the non-biblical sacraments, proliferation of sacramentals, use of images, cult of the saints, liturgical processions, masses for the dead—Catholics responded by reasserting the spiritual value of such rites, producing more processions, more elaborate decorations for churches, more side altars, more images, more magnificent music, more bejeweled chalices, richer liturgical vestments, even more saints. The pietistic trend consisted not just in the enforcement of liturgical uniformity but in the elaboration of a distinctively Catholic ritual vocabulary that contrasted with Protestant rituals, especially in the emphasis placed on the miracles of the saints and the Eucharist." *Ritual in Early Modern Europe*, 225.

[8] Mark R. Francis, "Liturgy and Popular Piety in a Historical Perspective," 39–42 in *Directory on Popular Piety and the Liturgy: Principles and Guidelines: A Commentary*, ed. Peter C. Phan (Collegeville, MN: Liturgical Press, 2005).

[9] Here Francis quotes the work of Marie Helène Froechlé-Chopard, "Les Dévotions populaires d'après les visites pastorales: Un Example: le Diocèse de Vence au début du XVIIIe siècle," *Revue d'histoire de l'église de France* 60 (1974): 85:100, at 85–86. Quoted in Francis, "Liturgy and Popular Piety," 39.

He further divides the first type of piety, the popular, into three moments of development: (1) sacred places such as mountaintops, springs, caves, and pilgrimage centers; (2) the emphasis on the power of more universal saints and of the Virgin Mary; and (3) the emphasis on the passion of Jesus Christ. On the other hand, the second type of piety, the official, emphasized "the importance of the sacraments," and hence "the mediatory power of the priesthood and of the official church." In his attempt to interrelate both types of piety, Francis writes:

> These two pieties did not necessarily oppose each other and at times overlapped, although the clergy tended to cast a jaundiced eye on some of the superstitious elements attached to the "popular" pre-Tridentine piety, especially those practices that emphasized that all had equal access to miraculous intercession without the direction and mediation of the hierarchical church.[10]

In sum, the "vigorous ecclesiology" from above that emerged from the Council of Trent developed into two types of popular religious practices, one stressing the sacramental and mediatory power of the official church and the other emphasizing "the popular" as it was practiced by the laity and often viewed with suspicion by the clergy. There was a concerted effort to centralize ("Romanize") these types of European devotionalism as a means to control both types of popular religious practices and create a distinctively Catholic ritual vocabulary in response to the Protestant reformers.[11]

[10] "Liturgy and Popular Piety," 40.

[11] In his more recent work Francis notes the impact of the printing press as "European culture moved from a premodern to modern worldview" during this period. He writes: "The challenge of Protestantism to the authority of the Church made possible by printing and more common literacy promoted more precise distinctions to be made between official (liturgical) worship and popular religious practice. It also produced a real change in the way in which people (both Catholics and Protestants) were engaged with at worship. No longer was the 'kinesthetic' or 'bodily' participation in the rites of the Church and in popular devotions the key mode of participation." Mark R. Francis, *Local Worship, Global Church: Popular Religion and the Liturgy* (Collegeville, MN: Liturgical Press, 2014), 138.

Another important factor contributing to this dialogue was the ritual disengagement of the laity during eucharistic celebrations. From this ecclesial context a liturgical renewal, known as the liturgical movement, began to develop during the nineteenth century, promoting the active participation of the laity during official liturgies.

The Eucharist as Source and Summit in the Writings of the Liturgical Movement

Throughout the span of the liturgical movement certain ecclesial leaders and liturgical scholars, in their concern for relating official liturgy with Christian life, used the image of the liturgy as source and summit in order to promote more lay participation during official liturgy and, further, to reorder the relationship between Eucharist and popular religious practices. But as the movement progressed, the vigorous promotion of the Eucharist by these pioneers also led to a decreased encouragement of popular religious practices. The following are summaries of the various approaches to understanding the place of liturgy as summit and source in relation to Christian life as it had been understood by some of the pioneers of the movement.

Dom Prosper Guéranger:
Liturgy as Social Prayer, Source, and Highest Form of Expression

The Benedictine monk Prosper Guéranger (1805–1875) believed that a liturgical renewal could be achieved by returning to the historical roots of liturgical, biblical, and patristic scholarship. Francis notes:

> [Guéranger] is considered the "founder" of the liturgical movement because he proposed the liturgy as *the principal source* for an ecclesial spirituality for both ordained and nonordained that went beyond looking at Catholic liturgy as only a series of rites whose rubrical directives had to be followed.[12]

---

[12] *Local Worship, Global Church*, 135. Emphasis added.

37

In the opening section of Guéranger's comprehensive study of the liturgy, *Institutions Liturgiques* (1841, hereafter, *IL*[13]), he inter-related liturgy with all other forms of prayer by viewing it as social prayer as distinct from individual prayer.[14] More specifically, liturgy imbues all other forms of prayer with more power and efficacy and is *a* source for poetic expression toward God who is *the* object and source of all forms of prayer.[15] Thus he regards liturgy as the *highest form* of expression ("*l'expression la plus haute*").[16] It is through the Eucharist that Christians "enter into" the paschal mystery, which is the "center" of the "supernatural life."[17]

Pope Leo XIII:
Christ Is the Life, and the Source of that Life Is the Eucharist
The liturgical academic scholarship that emerged from monastic liturgical centers in Europe throughout this time period would eventually receive affirmation at the official level by the turn of the twentieth century. On May 28, 1902, Pope Leo XIII (1810–1903) issued the encyclical *Mirae Caritatis* (hereafter *MC*). The encyclical is entirely devoted to the Eucharist, and its second section is entitled "The Source of Life" (articles 4–6).[18] During the period of Romanization of European devotionalism in the latter part of the nineteenth century, when practices of popular piety were perceived to be displacing official liturgy as a significant part of the worship life of the laity, Leo XIII stressed that Christ is "the Way, the Truth, and the Life,"[19] and that the source of that life is found in the Eucharist, from which flow the benefits of redemption. While he acknowledges that it is only *in God* and *through Jesus Christ* that

---

[13] *Institutions Liturgiques* (Paris: Société Génerale de Librairies Catholique, 1878).

[14] Ibid., 1.1.

[15] Ibid., 1.4.

[16] Ibid., 1.2.

[17] *L'Année Liturgique, Le Temps Pascal, Tome I* (Paris: *Librairie Religieuse H. Oudin*, 1909), 19–20.

[18] Available at http://www.vatican.va/holy_father/leo_xiii/encyclicals/documents/hf_l-xiii_enc_28051902_mirae-caritatis_en.html.

[19] *Mirae Caritatis* 1 (quoting John 14:6).

people receive "every best and choicest gift," it is the Eucharist that remains the source and chief gift through which Christians receive the means to nourish their lives.[20]

Pope Pius X: Liturgy as the Highest Form of Praise and Its Foremost and Indispensable Source

In 1903, Pope Pius X (1835–1914) promulgated his *motu propio, The Restoration of Church Music* (*Tra le Sollecitudini*, hereafter *TLS*).[21] The goal of *TLS* was to regulate the use of sacred music during liturgy and assert the primacy of Gregorian Chant as "the supreme model for sacred music."[22] The pope placed this concern within the larger issue of worshipers' "decorum" during liturgical celebrations performed in "the House of God, " thus implying a distinction between worship within church buildings and worship that occurs outside. We acquire "the true Christian spirit" when we actively participate in the holy mysteries, those public and solemn prayers of the church that are celebrated in the House of God. It is because of this participation that liturgy is the "foremost and indispensable source" for the Christian spirit.[23] While the larger goal of the encyclical was to restore the place of Gregorian Chant within liturgical celebrations, the pivotal phrase that called for the

[20] "For as men [sic] and states alike necessarily have their being from God, so they can do nothing good except in God through Jesus Christ, through whom every best and choicest gift has ever proceeded and proceeds. But the source and chief of all these gifts is the venerable Eucharist, which not only nourishes and sustains that life the desire whereof demands our most strenuous efforts, but also enhances beyond measure that dignity of man [sic] of which in these days we hear so much." *MC*, 6.

[21] Pope Pius X, *Tra le Sollecitudini*, An Apostolic Letter issued "Motu Proprio," *ASS* 36 (22 November 1903), 3–10 in *The New Liturgy: A Documentation, 1903–1965*, ed. R. Kevin Seasoltz (New York: Herder and Herder 1966).

[22] Ibid., 3.

[23] "It being our ardent desire to see the true Christian spirit restored in every respect and be preserved by all the faithful, we deem it necessary to provide before everything else for the sanctity and dignity of the temple, in which the faithful assemble for the object of acquiring this spirit from its foremost and indispensable fount (*fons*), which is the active participation in the holy mysteries and in the public and solemn prayer of the Church." Seasoltz, 4.

active participation of the laity was eventually highlighted by those who were more concerned with the pastoral implementation of the movement.

It is important for our purposes to mention another document by Pius X, *Sacra Tridentina Synodus* (1905, "On Frequent and Daily Reception of Holy Communion," hereafter *STS*). *STS* addressed the practice of yearly reception of communion by the laity. This decree not only discouraged this minimum requirement but went further and urged daily reception:

> Frequent and daily Communion, as a practice most earnestly desired by Christ our Lord and by the Catholic Church, should be open to all the faithful of whatever rank and condition of life; so that no one who is in the state of grace, and who approaches the holy table with a right and devout intention, can be prohibited therefrom.[24]

The promotion of daily communion indicates the lack of attendance and participation in official liturgy in the everyday lives of the laity. It also constitutes a privileging of daily Eucharist over and above all other everyday practices of popular religion. *STS* is an example of the larger Romanization and clericalization that was beginning to solidify at the start of the movement, as observed by Mark Francis:

> While most of the liturgical pioneers opposed the exaggerated emotionalism and individualism of devotions that had been approved by the church, they proposed the liturgy, renewed and taught to the people, as a more helpful way to "bring all things into one in Christ" ("*Instaurare* [*omnia*] *in Christo*," the motto of Pius X) and better able to impart the need for obedience to the universal tradition and discipline of the Roman church as expressed by the central authority in Rome.[25]

---

[24] Pius X, Decree of the Sacred Congregation of the Council, *Sacra Tridentina Synodus*, ASS 38 (December 22, 1905). Seasoltz, 13.

[25] "Liturgy and Popular Piety in a Historical Perspective," 42.

Dom Lambert Beauduin:
Liturgy, the True Prayer of the Church, as Source and Summit

Early in the twentieth century there was a growing and developing concern over the interrelationship between liturgy and devotional and pietistic practices. The distinction between official liturgies and devotional exercises was articulated in a report to the Benedictine Order during a chapter held on July 5, 1909.[26] Two months later another Benedictine would deliver a public address that would forever change the direction of the movement. On September 26, 1909, Dom Lambert Beauduin (1873–1960) presented a report entitled "The True Prayer of the Church" to the National Congress of Catholic Action (*Congrès national des Oeuvres catholiques*) in Malines, Belgium. By calling liturgy the *true* prayer of the church, Beauduin was making a distinction between devotional practices and official liturgies.[27]

Beauduin focused on how liturgy could be a source of nourishment for the spiritual life that occurs *outside* of official worship practice. Taking his lead from Pius X, Beauduin, together with other Benedictines and leaders from Louvain, Belgium, launched a more intentionally driven pastoral liturgical movement. According

---

[26] Describing what transpired during that chapter, André Haquin writes: "The spiritual and liturgical life is examined next. The monks draw on the nourishment of their spiritual life in the liturgy of the church which must be preferred over pious and devotional exercises. When it is necessary, we must first dispense with these exercises and not the conventual liturgy. The prayer could be seen as a personal preparation for Mass and Office. The choir of the church should be reserved for liturgical celebrations; spiritual exercises such as rosary could be done elsewhere." André Haquin, "Dom L. Beauduin et le Congrès des Oeuvres Catholiques de Malines: A l'occasion du centenaire du Mouvement liturgique belge (1909–2009)," *Questions Liturgiques* 91 (2010): 18–36, at 18 (author's translation).

[27] Haquin writes: "The expression 'true prayer of the church' means that it is an essential ('true') step of the church and that the liturgical 'prayer' is the response to God who is made known by Revelation. He developed his point as if it were a forgotten truth that should be brought back in promotion of the many lay Christians present at the Congress. This 'true prayer of the Church' which is the liturgy, implicitly means devotions cannot 'steal' this privileged place." Ibid., 25 (author's translation).

to Keith Pecklers, one of the goals of this pastorally focused movement was "to develop a liturgical spirituality where the Christian life is lived out of the font of the liturgy."[28] Beauduin vigorously promoted the idea that "the first and indispensable source of the true Christian spirit is the active participation of the faithful in the liturgy of the Church."[29] Like Pius X, he believed that it is only when Christians are able to participate actively *in the liturgy* that the liturgy becomes a source for "the true Christian spirit" *outside of the liturgy.*[30]

[28] Pecklers names four shared goals altogether: "(1) to work on liturgical texts: to translate *The Roman Missal* and to encourage its use as a devotional as well as liturgical book; to adapt the liturgical texts (at least for the Sunday Eucharist and Vespers) so that they were more pastorally accessible; (2) to develop a liturgical spirituality where the Christian life is lived out of the font of the liturgy. . . . (3) to cultivate the use of Gregorian chant within the liturgy, according to the wishes of Pius X . . . (4) to propose that those entrusted with ministry of music in parishes, i.e., music directors and their choirs, should set aside time each year for a retreat in monasteries or other liturgical centers." Keith Peckers, *The Unread Vision: The Liturgical Movement in the United States of America: 1926–1955* (Collegeville, MN: Liturgical Press, 1998), 13.

[29] "The first and indispensable source of the true Christian spirit is found in the active participation of the faithful in the liturgy of the church. Such is the truth that was developed by Pius X in his first pontifical act. Now, to bring about this result, two major means present themselves: the intelligence of the liturgical texts and the collective chant of the faithful." Lambert Beauduin, "La Vraie Prière de L'Église: Rapport présenté par le R. P. Dom Lambert Beaudoin O.S.B.," *Questions Liturgiques* 91 (2010): 37–41 (author's translation).

[30] Other writings by Beauduin would continue this interplay, including most notably his only book, *La Piété de l'Église*, which would later be translated as *Liturgy: the Life of the Church*. He writes: "What are these priestly and hierarchical acts, the primary and indispensable source of Christian life? . . . It is the sanctifying mission of the Catholic hierarchy (*munus ministerii*—the mission of the ministry) to make of us living and holy oblations, offered daily unto the glory of the Father, in union with the unique sacrifice of Jesus Christ—a mission that is destined to extend all the divine energies of the eternal priesthood unto all generations." Dom Lambert Beauduin, *Liturgy the Life of the Church*, 3d ed., trans. Virgil Michel (Collegeville, MN: Liturgical Press, 2002; first pub. 1914), 13–14.

Virgil Michel:
Liturgy, the Life of the Church, as Source for Social Activism

After studying throughout Europe from 1921 to 1925, and specifically under Beauduin at San Anselmo in Rome, the American Benedictine Virgil Michel (1890–1938) returned home to the United States to Saint John's Abbey in Collegeville, Minnesota, in 1926. Michel's writings demonstrate the interplay between participation during official liturgies and participation in social activism that occurs *outside* liturgy. He wrote during the 1930s, a time when "liturgically-based social activism" began to emerge in the United States.[31] His concern for the relationship between liturgy and social justice found inspiration in Leo XIII's encyclical *On Capital and Labor* (*Rerum Novarum*, 1891), considered to be the first official legislation helping to inaugurate the modern Roman Catholic teaching and practice of social justice. But rather than limit Leo's vision to the everyday realm of labor, Michel wanted to extend this notion of justice to include all aspects of social life and connect all of these aspects to the liturgy. He found theological grounding in the theological doctrine of Mystical Body of Christ[32] and viewed the liturgy, particularly the Eucharist, as *the very life of the church*[33] that is marked by acts of social justice.

[31] Before this period, "[d]uring the 1920s," as Pecklers writes, "religious individualism dominated much of Catholic life and piety in the United States. In retrospect, it is not surprising that there was little recognition of the Eucharist as a common act of worship (that is, as fundamentally social in nature) because a good number of Catholics failed to recognize their own relationship to one another as brothers and sisters—as members of that same living body of Christ." *The Unread Vision*, 26.

[32] Many found inspiration regarding this doctrine in the writings of Johann Adam Möhler (1798–1838), who retrieved the Pauline notion of the Body of Christ and emphasized the "organic unity" of the church by promoting a view that the church was similar to a living organism, and not so much an organization that members simply joined and where they did their Sunday duty week by week. See *The Unread Vision*, 30.

[33] Michel's English translation of the title of Beauduin's book, *La Piété de l'Église* ("The Piety of the Church"), as *Liturgy: the Life of Church* is demonstrative of this conviction.

Pope Pius XII: Practices of Popular Devotion Alongside Official Liturgy, Christ as Source, and the Eucharist as Culmination

As the liturgical movement progressed to include other countries throughout the 1930s and 1940s ("the internationalization of the movement"),[34] consensus began to grow with regard to liturgical changes. The writings and visions of the early liturgical pioneers would continue through ongoing development in theological and historical scholarship, liturgical publication, national and regional gatherings, and pastoral promotion. During these decades the restoration goals that had marked the early stages of the movement began to focus more on liturgical reform.[35] Two official documents were promulgated during the 1950s during the pontificate of Pius XII (1939–1958): *The Mystical Body of Christ* (*Mystici Corporis Christi*, 1943) and *The Sacred Liturgy* (*Mediator Dei*, 1947). The encyclical *Mystici Corporis Christi* (hereafter MCC), affirmed the theological trajectory that had been developing throughout the movement and set the ecclesial framework that would later be articulated in Vatican II's *Lumen Gentium*. The encyclical's use of the term "source" (*fons*) more often referred to Jesus Christ and not to the eucharistic liturgy.[36] While popular devotions are acknowledged as being practiced alongside official liturgy, nevertheless, it is in the Eucharist that the Mystical Body of Christ on earth reaches a unitive culmination (*culmen*) with Christ the Head and that the *sacrifice* of the Mass becomes the culmination of the entire Mass.[37]

---

[34] Haquin, "The Liturgical Movement and Catholic Ritual Revision," 704.

[35] See James White, *Roman Catholic Worship: Trent to Today* (Collegeville, MN: Liturgical Press, 2003).

[36] There are instances in which the pope refers to Jesus Christ (and *not* the liturgy) as the "source," including Christ as the "supernatural source," as "the source whence the grace of the Holy Spirit should flow unto all the children of the first parent" (art. 9); "Holiness begins from Christ; and Christ is its cause. For no act conducive to salvation can be performed unless it proceeds from Him as from its supernatural source" (art. 51); "If we examine closely this divine principle of life and power given by Christ, insofar as it constitutes the very source of every gift and created grace" (art. 56). Pope Pius XII, encyclical letter *Mystici Corporis Christi, AAS* 35 (29 June 1943), in Seasoltz, ed., *The New Liturgy*.

[37] Ibid., 66.

Mediator Dei (hereafter *MD*) affirmed many of the theological, academic, and pastoral trajectories of the liturgical movement and solidified more fully the place of the Eucharist in relation to all other pious activities. Liturgy is a form of public worship that the entire Mystical Body of Christ (head and members) renders to God. While the sacraments are a source (*fons*) of grace for all other pious activities, the Eucharist, as the chief act of divine worship, is the source *and center* of those activities.[38] Thus, while the Eucharist is considered to be "a sacrament of devotion," it remains the *source and center* of all other forms of Christian piety. Finally, *MD* specifically nuanced this language by stating that the *mystery* of the Holy Eucharist is *the head and center* of Christian religion and that the *sacrifice* of the Mass is the culmination point of the entire celebration.[39]

Summary

From the start of the liturgical movement, one of the chief concerns of its pioneers was the relationship between liturgy and Christian life. As a way to articulate this relationship the ecclesial leaders and liturgical scholars of the movement sought to relate official liturgy, especially the Eucharist, with all other practices of popular religion by promoting diverse images of the Eucharist as source and summit, as a means to renew the active participation of the laity during liturgy and at the same time to maintain

---

[38] *MD* 66: "The mystery of the most holy Eucharist which Christ, the High Priest instituted, and which he commands to be continually renewed in the Church by his ministers, is the culmination [*caput*] and center, as it were, of the Christian religion. We consider it opportune in speaking about the crowning act of the sacred liturgy to delay for a little while and call your attention, venerable brethren, to this most important subject." Ibid., 126.

[39] *MD* 114: "They, therefore, err from the path of truth who do not want to have Masses celebrated unless the faithful communicate; and those are still more in error who, in holding that it is altogether necessary for the faithful to receive holy communion as well as the priest, put forward the captious argument that here there is question not of a sacrifice merely, but of a sacrifice and a supper of brotherly union, and consider the general communion of all present as the culminating point of the whole celebration." Ibid., 137.

hierarchical control over all types of worship practices. Guéranger interrelated all types of Christian prayer, namely, the public prayer of official liturgy and the prayerful life that occurs *outside of liturgy* in "the social state." Pius X placed more emphasis on boundaries by focusing on official liturgy as the common, public, and solemn prayer of the church that occurs within "the House of God" and called on the laity to participate actively in the solemn prayers of the church. It is because of this participation that liturgy is the "foremost and indispensable source" for the Christian spirit. Furthermore, his encyclical, *STS*, which encouraged the daily reception of the Eucharist, heightened the prominence of the Eucharist in the everyday lives of Christians. Pope Leo XIII, Lambert Beauduin, Virgil Michel, and Pope Pius XII interrelated the terms "liturgy" or "the Eucharist" with "Christian life": for example, "the true Christian spirit," "the life of the church," "the supernatural life," and so on. The various terms for "Christian life" throughout these writings demonstrate the breadth of Christian worship activities, which would eventually be hierarchically reordered through a process of Romanization and centralization as a means to maintain control over these practices in relation to official liturgies. Inspired by the encyclicals *On Capital and Labor* and *The Restoration of Church Music*, Michel further broadened the spectrum of Christian life by vigorously promoting the active participation of the laity during official liturgy in order that the entire church might, in turn, participate in practices of social justice that he hoped would transpire as a form of worship beyond the boundaries of liturgical celebrations.

Vatican II and Post-Conciliar Documents on the Relationship between the Eucharist as the Source and Summit of Christian Life and Popular Religious Practices

For Jude Penland, the 10:30 AM Mass is "The Show," a term used in baseball. The physical therapist for the San Francisco Giants continues:

> It's a term in baseball: when you work in the minor leagues and you work your way up . . . you get to play in the Major League. It's called "being in the show." So I call the 10:30 "The Show." A lot of baseball metaphors pop up in my conversations.

Our interview was taking place in my office at Old St. Mary's Cathedral in Chinatown, since St. Francis Hospital, her other place of employment, was conveniently located a few blocks away. Jude told me about her search for a spiritual connection and her discovery of St. Agnes parish. When she "walked into 'that' area," [the hospitality area], she immediately felt "a sudden connection . . . a big serious connection!" She soon discovered the Jesuit intellectual tradition and eventually was received into the Roman Catholic Church. The 10:30 AM Mass is "The Show" because after years of experiencing her "spiritual dryness" she finally "connected" with the community and the liturgies at St. Agnes.

❖　❖　❖

In this chapter I focus on how the image of "the Eucharist as source and summit" came to be articulated in the documents of the Second Vatican Council, as well as in some of the post-conciliar statements by Popes John Paul II and Benedict XVI, while demonstrating that, despite a more pronounced reordering between official liturgy and non-official worship practices, a fluidity of interactions between these two poles has remained. By the time the council convened on October 11, 1962, there was a sufficient supply of historical, official, and theological resources to correlate the components involved in asserting that official liturgy, particularly the Eucharist, was the source and summit of Christian life. On December 4, 1963, the council promulgated its first document, the Constitution on the Sacred Liturgy (*Sacrosanctum Concilium*, hereafter SC). One year later, on November 21, 1964, the council issued the Dogmatic Constitution on the Church (*Lumen Gentium*, hereafter LG), followed a year later by the promulgation of the Decree on the Ministry and Life of Priests (*Presbyterorum Ordinis*, hereafter PO) on December 7, 1965. These three documents employ the terms "fount" and "summit" in their description of official liturgy, for example:

> SC 10: The liturgy is the summit toward which the activity of the Church is directed; it is also the fount from which all her power flows.[1]

> LG 11: Taking part in the eucharistic sacrifice, which is the fount and summit of the whole Christian life, they offer the Divine Victim to God, and offer themselves along with It.[2]

> PO 5: In this light, the Eucharist shows itself as the source and the summit of the whole work of preaching the Gospel.[3]

---

[1] Constitution on the Sacred Liturgy, 1–30 in *The Liturgy Documents: A Parish Resource*, 4th ed. (Chicago: Liturgy Training Publications, 2004).

[2] Dogmatic Constitution on the Church, 1–95 in *Vatican Council II: The Basic Sixteen Documents*, ed. Austin Flannery (Northport, NY: Costello Publishing Company, 1996).

[3] Decree on the Ministry and Life of Priests, in ibid., 317–64.

Note the transitional changes of terms, from "the liturgy" in SC to "the eucharistic sacrifice" in LG to "the Eucharist" in PO. This sequence demonstrates that, by the end of the council, the hierarchical order of worship practices had become solidified in official teaching, placing the Eucharist at the top of the worship pyramid while ordering all other activities of Christian life, including non-official worship practices, below.

This chapter is divided into three parts. In the first I provide a commentary on articles 5–13 of SC, including a brief background of the subcommission that wrote the first draft of those articles. Taken as a whole, the articles set the larger framework for how the council participants came to address the relationship between liturgy and Christian life. I will provide a more detailed examination of the pivotal article 10, the first of the council documents to image the liturgy as summit and source, and will include an examination of its surrounding articles that considers, albeit briefly, the place of popular devotions in relation to official liturgy. In the next part I provide a commentary on the other two articles in council documents that reference article 10 of SC, namely, article 11 of LG and article 5 of PO. These nuanced rearticulations of article 10 of SC demonstrate the continued need to interrelate official liturgy and non-official worship practices, particularly the role relationships between the clergy and the laity in the performance of all worship practices. Finally, in the third part I examine some writings by John Paul II and Benedict XIV with regard to these questions, including John Paul II's *The Day of the Lord* (1998) and *The Church from the Eucharist* (2003), and Benedict XVI's *The Sacrament of Charity* (2007). By the end of the chapter we will see that the many uses of the terms "source" and "summit" can best be described as broadly scattered yet significant in the church's ongoing reflection on the relationship between liturgy and popular religious practices.

Articles 5–13 of the Constitution on the Sacred Liturgy

*The Formation of the Subcommission on Liturgy and the
Life of the Church*

On November 12, 1960, the preparatory liturgical commission of the Second Vatican Council met for the first time. The initial task of the commission was to organize and divide its members into sub-commissions based on various aspects of the liturgy. That the relationship between liturgy and Christian life was a major concern in the early drafts of *SC* became apparent in the development of its most important subcommission, *The Mystery of the Sacred Liturgy and its Relation to the Life of the Church*. At first this subcommission did not exist. Instead, the sixty-five members and consultors were subdivided into twelve subcommissions:

The Mass

Sacramental Concelebration

Divine Office

Sacraments and Sacramentals

Revision of the Calendar

Use of Latin

Liturgical Formation

Participation of the Faithful in the Sacred Liturgy

Linguistic Adaptation to the Tradition and Ethos of Peoples

Simplification of Liturgical Vestments

Sacred Music

Sacred Art

On November 15, Cardinal Giulio Bevilacqua suggested that a thirteenth subcommission be formed to write a "theological-ascetical chapter on the mystery of the liturgy and the life of the Church."[4] The members of the new subcommission included Bevilacqua (Relator) and Cipriano Vagaggini (Secretary), and the consultors included Henri Jenny, Joseph Jungmann, Giovanni Cannizzaro, Ignacio Oñatibia, Herman Schmidt, and Ansgar Dirks. The subcommission's work led to the writing of the first chapter of SC. As Bugnini observed: "Little by little . . . the chapter grew more substantial and became the most important part of the entire Con-

[4] Annibale Bugnini, *The Reform of the Liturgy: 1948–1975* (Collegeville, MN: Liturgical Press, 1990), 17.

stitution; to the theological and ascetical aspects were added the pastoral and the normative."[5] Throughout the next two years, various titles for this chapter were proposed, including: "The Mystery of the Sacred Liturgy in the Life of the Church" (November 1960), "The General Promotion and Restoration of the Sacred Liturgy" (April 1961), "The General Principles for the Restoration and Promotion of the Sacred Liturgy" (November 1961), and "The General Principles for the Restoration and Promotion of the Liturgy" (January 1962). Eventually the first chapter was entitled "General Principles for the Restoration and Promotion of the Sacred Liturgy." The first proposed title included the term "the Life of the Church," which was removed in the second proposal. However, "the Life of the Church" would be reinserted under the subtitle of the first section of this chapter, "The Nature of the Sacred Liturgy and Its Importance in the Church's Life." This section further divides into two parts: a theological exposition of liturgy (articles 5–8) and the relationship between liturgy and church life (articles 9–13).

Articles 5–8: A Theological Exposition of Liturgy

Article 5 articulates a liturgical theology that recounts salvation history through the prism of the paschal mystery (*mysterium paschale*). Rather than employing dogmatic statements to expound on the meaning of the paschal mystery, the writers of SC chose to employ scriptural references from the Old and New Testaments. In short, Christ achieved the work of redemption through his passion, death, and resurrection and thus the "sacrament of the whole Church" was born.

Article 6 recounts *how* the mystery of Christ is revealed in the life of the church. Christ sent out his apostles to preach the gospel "that they might accomplish the work of salvation . . . by means of sacrifice and sacraments . . . around which the entire liturgical life of the Church revolves." In this passage the life of the church is said to be brought about through the twofold mission of the

---

[5] Ibid.

proclamation of the Gospel and the mediation of this proclamation through sacrifice and sacraments. The article's statement that "the entire liturgical life of the Church" revolves around "sacrifice and sacraments" points back to past metaphors that viewed liturgy as a "central act" of the church.

In his commentary on the constitution, Josef A. Jungmann notes that the preliminary schema only listed "sacraments" in this section and not sacrifice. However, a distinction was made between "the Eucharist" (within which the sacrifice of the Mass occurs) and the other sacraments and sacramentals.[6] This distinction is structurally demonstrated in the division of chapters within SC. For example, chapter 2 is entirely devoted to the Eucharist, while chapter 3 speaks of "The Other Sacraments and the Sacramentals." This pattern demonstrates a hierarchical ordering of meaning behind the term "the liturgy" within official documents: while "the liturgy of the Church" denotes all ecclesial acts of official worship (the sacraments, the Liturgy of the Hours, and so on), it is clear that official statements on the liturgy place more emphasis on the *eucharistic liturgy*.[7] Further, Jungmann points out that the preparatory commission intentionally avoided any *one definition* of the liturgy as they felt such a task should be left to "academic discussions."[8] In short, the term "the sacred liturgy" as used in SC covers all official ecclesial acts of worship, within which the eucharistic liturgy holds pride of place.

The issue of how to articulate the privileging of the Eucharist over and above the other sacraments was also a cause of concern during the debates that ensued around article 7. This article articulated the manifold ways of Christ's presence and stated that Christ is "always present in His Church," but gives special emphasis to

[6] Josef Andreas Jungmann, "Constitution on the Sacred Liturgy," in *Commentary on the Documents of Vatican II*, vol. 1, ed. Herbert Vorgrimler (New York: Herder and Herder, 1967), 12.

[7] Recall that the *Catechism of the Catholic Church* made similar analogies when it described the Eucharist as "a fountain" and the other sacraments as "rivulets" ("small streams"). See n. 2 above.

[8] Jungmann, "Constitution on the Sacred Liturgy," 13.

Christ's presence in the church's liturgical celebrations, and particularly in the Eucharist. The naming of the fourfold presence of Christ followed:

> He is present in the sacrifice of the Mass, not only in the person of His minister, "the same now offering, through the ministry of priests, who formerly offered himself on the cross," but especially under the eucharistic species. By His power He is present in the sacraments, so that when a man baptizes it is really Christ Himself who baptizes. He is present in His word, since it is He Himself who speaks when the holy scriptures are read in the Church. He is present, lastly, when the Church prays and sings, for He promised: "Where two or three are gathered together in my name, there am I in the midst of them" (Matt. 18:20).

Critical objections arose over this article. "[T]he resistance was caused principally by the anxiety that faith in the eucharistic presence could be belittled."[9] In defense of the final form of the article, Jungmann writes: "The resistance evidently sprang from a theological school of thought little accustomed to conceiving the continued existence of the Lord in his transfigured humanity in the glory of the Father as his primary manner of being, which operates fully in all other modes of his presence, even though in different ways."[10]

Article 8 introduces new imagery that contributes to our investigation of the relationship between liturgy and Christian life. It articulates the relationship between "the earthly liturgy" and "the heavenly liturgy . . . toward which we journey as pilgrims, where Christ is sitting at the right hand of God, a minister of the holies and of the true tabernacle." The former liturgy provides "a foretaste" of the latter. For our purposes the use of the image of pilgrimage is important to consider, because it provides a larger eschatological framework. While this imagery does not use the terms "fount and summit" (these will appear in the next article),

[9] Ibid., 13.
[10] Ibid.

nevertheless, the introduction of the larger eschatological dimension of the earthly and heavenly liturgies is vital as we consider the relationships between these types of liturgies and Christian life.

Articles 9–13: The Relationship Between Liturgy and Church Life

The second half of section 1 includes articles 9–13. While article 8 focuses on the earthly and heavenly liturgies within a larger eschatological framework, article 9 complements this perspective by considering *all other activities* of the church:

> The liturgy does not exhaust the entire activity of the Church. Before people can come to the liturgy they must be called to faith and to conversion. . . .
>
> Therefore the Church announces the good tidings of salvation to those who do not believe, so that all may know the true God and Jesus Christ whom He has sent, and may be converted from their ways, doing penance. To believers also the Church must ever preach faith and penance, she must prepare them for the sacraments, teach them to observe all that Christ has commanded, and invite them to all the works of charity, worship, and the apostolate. For all these works make it clear that Christ's faithful, though not of this world, are to be the light of the world and to glorify the Father in the eyes of all.

Article 9 moves beyond liturgical activity to include other activities of evangelization, discipleship, and mission. These include: (1) the announcing of salvation, (2) the preaching of faith and penance, (3) preparation for the sacramental life, (4) the teaching of Christ's commandments, and (5) inviting nonbelievers to the activities of charity, piety, and the apostolate. Believers of the faith perform these activities so as to move unbelievers toward becoming living members of the faith.

Article 10

After naming the activities within the church's activity that fit into the larger framework of Christian life, article 10 then places these activities in relation to the liturgy:

Still, the liturgy is the summit [*culmen*] toward which the activity of the Church [*actio Ecclesiae*] is directed [*tendit*]; at the same time it is the fount [*fons*] from which all the Church's power flows. For the aim and object of apostolic works is that all who are made children of God by faith and baptism should come together to praise God in the midst of his Church, to take part in the Sacrifice, and to eat the Lord's Supper. For the aim and object of apostolic works is that all who are made children of God by faith and baptism should come together to praise God in the midst of his Church, to take part in the sacrifice, and to eat the Lord's Supper.

The liturgy in its turn moves the faithful, filled with "the paschal sacraments" to be "one in holiness"; it prays that "they may hold fast in their lives to what they have grasped by their faith"; the renewal in the Eucharist of the covenant between the Lord and his people draws the faithful into the compelling love of Christ and sets them on fire. From the liturgy, therefore, particularly the Eucharist, grace is poured forth upon us as from a fountain; the liturgy is the source for achieving in the most effective way possible human sanctification and God's glorification, the end to which all the Church's other activities are directed.

The movement from article 9 to article 10 is critical for understanding how the Council related the liturgy to the fivefold activities previously mentioned: namely, in addition to the activities of announcing, preaching, preparing, teaching, and inviting, all other activities of the church reach their summit (*culmen*) in the liturgy. *At the same time*, the liturgy is the fount from which the power of the church flows (the "her" refers to the church: "*eius virtus emanat.*"). By combining the two terms used for describing the liturgy (summit and fount) into one sentence, article 10 not only describes *what* the liturgy is but also suggests an intrinsic twofold relational movement between one and the other (*et simul*). Thus the activity of the church leads to and culminates in the liturgy, which simultaneously leads to the outpouring of the church's power.

The connection between summit and fount becomes more apparent in the rest of the article. Here "apostolic works" (*labores apostolici*) has as its goal (is directed toward, *ad id ordinantur*) the physical coming together in prayer *in the midst of [the] church*, that is, within official worship space where the eucharistic sacrifice and the eating of the body and blood of Christ take place. This "coming together" *in its turn* (*vicissim*) moves the faithful toward the establishment of unity among them. Here the two directions suggest two goals: apostolic endeavor (the activity of the church) culminates at the liturgy and, as a result, the liturgy "moves the faithful" (*impellit fideles*) toward unity. Perhaps a better translation of "*impellit*" is "impels": that is, liturgy does not simply "move" the faithful but does so with some driving force or sense of urgency.

This last movement, the liturgy impeling the faithful toward unity, is further specified in what follows. Liturgy "fills" the faithful with "the paschal sacraments" in order that they may be one in holiness. *From* the liturgy, and *especially* from the Eucharist, grace is derived and, *with greatest efficacy*, obtained (for us) in Christ. All other activities of the church (and here we particularly highlight the fivefold activities in article 9) are directed toward human sanctification in Christ and the glorification of God *as their end*.

To summarize the second half of this article, then, liturgy *impels* the faithful toward unity and, especially through the Eucharist, *provides* the greatest efficacy of grace so that all activities performed by Christians may be *directed* toward the twofold movement of human sanctification and the glorification of God as their end (i.e., the goal of the church's activity).

Articles 11–13

Articles 11–13 are relatively shorter than the previous articles of this section, but they remain important since they provide a further explanation of liturgical preparation and consider other spiritual practices that occur before and after liturgical celebrations. Despite the shorter length of these articles, it is important to review them and then place them in more intentional conversation with article 10.

Article 11 continues the theological thread begun in article 10 regarding "the full effects" of the liturgy. Specifically, it is a qualification of what is necessary for the effects of the liturgy to reach their full potential: namely, the proper dispositions of (1) attunement between mind and voice, and (2) cooperation with grace: "But in order that the liturgy may possess its full effectiveness, it is necessary that the faithful come to it with proper dispositions, that their minds be attuned to their voices, and that they cooperate with divine grace lest they receive it in vain." The article continues by noting a corresponding collaboration between the presider and the other participants during liturgy: "Pastors must therefore realize that when the liturgy is celebrated something more is required than the mere observation of the laws governing valid and lawful celebration; it is also their duty to ensure that the faithful take part fully aware of what they are doing, actively engaged in the rite, and enriched by its effects."

Presiders are called to move beyond the rubrical precisions contained within the rites in order to lead all participants toward active engagement or, as Jungmann explains, "an intelligent and fruitful participation."[11] Here we glimpse what is to follow in the next important section of SC (arts. 14–20), which focuses on the full, conscious, and active participation of the faithful during liturgy. Article 11 makes note of what ought to *precede* liturgy on the part of the faithful (their "proper dispositions") and what occurs within the liturgy that goes beyond mere observance of the rubrics (active engagement by the faithful), *which leads to* an enrichment of its effects.

Article 12 introduces another term to include under the larger umbrella of "Christian life," namely, "the spiritual life." It uses this term to move beyond the boundaries of what occurs *within* official and public liturgies and provides a list of prayerful examples:

> The spiritual life, however, is not limited solely to participation in the liturgy. Christians are indeed called to pray in union with each other, but they must also enter into their chamber to pray to the Father in secret; further, according to the teaching of the Apostle, they should pray without ceasing. We learn from the same Apostle that we must always bear about in our body the dying of Jesus, so that the life also of Jesus may be made manifest in our bodily

---

[11] Ibid., 16.

frame. This is why we ask the Lord in the sacrifice of the Mass that "receiving the offering of the spiritual victim," he may fashion us for himself "as an eternal gift."

A distinction is made between the spiritual life that is practiced in the liturgy and the spiritual life that is practiced outside liturgy, particularly as these practices are performed alone or "in secret," as distinct from other prayerful practices that occur with other Christians, but nonetheless remain outside liturgy. Note that no distinction is made between non-liturgical practices that are performed alone (for example, quiet meditation) and those performed alone yet technically remain *liturgical* (for example, the praying of the Liturgy of the Hours by oneself).

The second part of this article brings back the theme of the eucharistic sacrifice. In some ways it once again accents that all activities, specifically spiritual prayer forms, are to move toward the sacrificial offering that occurs during the Mass. This parallels the reference to the sacrifice of the Mass in article 10 and participation in this sacrifice as one of "the goals" of liturgy. The reintroduction here of sacrificial language will be echoed again in article 11 of LG.

This entire section draws to a close with article 13, which considers the place of popular devotions in relation to Christian life and the liturgy. Since this article comes after article 12, it seems to locate all popular religious practices as a further extension of "the spiritual life." Yet even here SC's presentation on popular devotions is more cautious when relating these practices to official liturgy:

> Popular devotions of the Christian people are to be highly endorsed, provided they accord with the laws and norms of the Church, above all when they are ordered by the Apostolic See.
>
> Devotions proper to particular churches also have a special dignity if they are undertaken by mandate of the bishops according to customs or books lawfully approved.
>
> But these devotions should be so fashioned that they harmonize with the liturgical seasons, accord with the sacred liturgy, are in

some way derived from it, and lead the people to it, since, in fact, the liturgy by its very nature far surpasses any of them.

Each affirmation of popular devotional practices is quickly followed by an affirmation of adherence to official laws and administration, thus offering a solid basis for Mark Francis's observation of the Romanization of Christian piety since the Council of Trent. Furthermore, their linkage to liturgy places devotions in a subservient position: they are not only to *harmonize* with the liturgy but *accord with* it because by its very nature it *far surpasses* them. Clearly, the qualification of "far" denotes a more acute attempt to reorder the degrees of distance between spiritual practices.

Article 11 of the Dogmatic Constitution on the Church and Article 5 of the Decree on the Ministry and Life of Priests

The image of liturgy as "summit and fount" made a lasting impression and exercised influence during the rest of the council as well as on all future documents and theological reflections that sought to articulate the relationship of liturgy and Christian life. Here I will comment on two articles from two other council documents: article 11 of LG and article 5 of PO. These nuanced rearticulations of article 10 of SC demonstrate the continued need to interrelate official liturgy and non-official worship practices, particularly the role relationships between clergy and laity in the performance of all worship practices.

Article 11 of the Dogmatic Constitution on the Church (LG): The Eucharistic Sacrifice and the Whole Christian Life

LG was written just one year after SC. Article 11 of LG reads: "Taking part in the eucharistic sacrifice, the source and summit of the Christian life, they [the faithful] offer the Divine Victim to God and themselves along with him." The difference between the articulation of article 10 of SC and article 11 of LG is striking. First, LG replaces the term "the liturgy" with "the eucharistic sacrifice." While the eucharistic sacrifice that occurs within the celebration of the Mass is liturgical, not all liturgies are eucharistic sacrifices. Previous articulations of this relationship expressed this dynamic by using the term "liturgy," followed by "especially the Eucharist."

What is being promoted here is a particular sacrificial theology, further solidifying the hierarchical ordering between the Eucharist and the other sacraments as well as all other popular religious practices and Christian activities or, in a simpler term, "Christian life." Pius XII's encyclicals, MCC and MD, stated that it is in the Eucharist that the Mystical Body of Christ on earth reaches a unitive culmination (*culmen*) with Christ the Head, and that the *sacrifice* of the Mass is the culmination of the entire Mass. Similarly, LG's location of *fons* is reduced to the particular act of Christ's sacrifice on the cross and our union with that sacrifice during eucharistic celebrations. We also saw similar references to the sacrifice of the Mass in article 12 of SC, which placed all spiritual activities performed by the laity in relation to this sacrifice. Thus, by extension, the use of sacrificial imagery continues the clericalizing trend of "official piety" from the nineteenth century, or, as Mark Francis wrote, "the mediatory power of the priesthood and of the official Church," in contrast to the "popular piety" of the laity.

Article 11 of LG is written within a larger theological context of its second chapter, entitled "The People of God" (arts. 9–17). It was within this section that a debate arose among the council participants about the proposed distinction between "the common priesthood of the faithful" and "the priesthood of the hierarchical ministry" (art. 10). In his commentary on LG, Aloys Grillmeier noted the misgivings among the council participants over the introduction of this concept, due to the fear "that the special status of the consecrated priesthood might be lost sight of."[12] However, as Grillmeier shows, the biblical foundations of the priesthood of believers, as well as past documents such as Pius XII's MD and the council's SC, provided the necessary foundation that led to the acceptance of this concept:

---

[12] Aloys Grillmeier, "The People of God," 153–85 in *Commentary on the Documents of Vatican II*, vol. 1, ed. Herbert Vorgrimler (New York: Herder and Herder, 1967), 156.

The consecrated priesthood is not to be understood merely as an intensification and heightening of the dignity and mission of the common priesthood, but represents a new type of priestly dignity and power, even though it is based on the common priesthood. But of their nature, the common and the special priesthood are ordained to each other, by virtue of their common participation in the priesthood of Christ, which, however, they share in a different way. Thus the two types of priesthood are to be defined in the light of their relationship to Christ the high priest.[13]

As a second modification, Article 11 of LG replaces "the activity of the Church" (from SC) with "the whole Christian life." The concern to articulate the relationship between liturgy and popular practices under the rubric of "Christian life" was found in the very first article of SC and subsequently spelled out the aims of the entire council:

This Sacred Council has several aims in view: it desires to impart an ever increasing vigor to the Christian life of the faithful; to adapt more suitably to the needs of our own times those institutions which are subject to change; to foster whatever can promote union among all who believe in Christ; to strengthen whatever can help to call the whole of humanity into the household of the Church. The Council therefore sees particularly cogent reasons for undertaking the reform and promotion of the liturgy.

The inclusion of the term "Christian life" ("*vitam christianam*") in article 1 of SC and article 11 of LG maintained one of the desired goals of the pioneers of the liturgical movement, namely, that the liturgy would impact the everyday life of Christians. Of the four goals the council names, note that particular concern for Christian life occupies the first position. In his commentary on articles 9–13 of SC, Jungmann further reemphasizes this goal, stating that the council maintained as its chief concern "the totality of ecclesial life—both the work of the church as well as the life of the individual."[14]

---

[13] Ibid., 158.
[14] Jungmann, "Constitution on the Sacred Liturgy," 14.

In the documents and writings we have examined thus far one may perceive that the terms "Christian life" and "church life" are interchangeable. More often than not, official documents will use ecclesial terms (for example, "the life of the church") when speaking about the people to whom the documents are addressed: for example, the laity, clergy, bishops, episcopal conferences, and so on. At other times the term "Christian life" is used to describe the spectrum of Christian life and activities.[15] The best example of this is "the *whole* of Christian life" in article 11 of LG. The insertion of this phrase is in keeping with the spirit of the entire document, which sought to articulate the ecclesial role and nature of the church within the larger context of the sociocultural world. As the introduction states:

> Christ is the Light of nations. . . . Since the Church, in Christ, is a sacrament—a sign and instrument, that is, of communion with God and of the unity of the entire human race—it here proposes, for the benefit of the faithful and of the entire world, to describe more clearly, and in the tradition laid down by earlier councils, its own nature and universal mission. The present situation lends greater urgency to this duty of the Church, so that all people, who nowadays are drawn ever more closely together by social, technical and cultural bonds, may achieve full unity in Christ.

A third modification between article 11 of LG and article 10 of SC may at first seem minor but, in my estimation, it is quite important. Article 11 of LG condenses "summit and fount" from article 10 of SC into a much shorter phrase. I suspect this may have contributed to its popular use thereafter. The best example of this comes from article 1324 of the 1992 *Catechism of the Catholic Church*. In its section devoted to the Eucharist a reference is made to LG and not to SC:

> The Eucharist is "the fount and summit of the Christian life" (*LG* 11). The other sacraments, and indeed all ecclesiastical ministries and works of the apostolate, are bound up with the Eucharist and are

[15] I prefer this term since it is more far-reaching and comprehensive in scope: the spectrum of Christian life and activities at times moves beyond ecclesial frameworks, as I will demonstrate in the second half of this book.

oriented toward it. For in the blessed Eucharist is contained the whole spiritual good of the Church, namely Christ himself, our Pasch.[16]

It is worth noting that even though there is a direct reference to LG there is still a modification in the phrase, the replacement of "the eucharistic sacrifice" with "the Eucharist." Finally, the reordering of terms might also go unnoticed; the terms in LG are switched around from their original order in SC. SC placed summit *before* fount; in LG the shortened phrase now reads "fount and summit." The reason for this reordering of the terms remains unclear. Does such a reordering place more emphasis on the *fons* over the *culmen*? And does such a reordering affect one's approach to understanding the Eucharist? In any case, the reordering of the terms and the condensing of article 10 of SC may also have contributed to the preference for citing article 10 of LG in future documents and writings.

Article 5 of the Decree on the Ministry and Life of Priests (PO):
The Function of the Priest in Relation to Source and Summit
    The last Vatican II document to consider is article 5 of the Decree on the Ministry and Life of Priests. This article fits within the first section of the second chapter, which addresses the priestly function of presbyters (arts. 4–6). Article 4 names the primary duty of the priests as that of proclaiming the Gospel:

> The people of God is formed into one in the first place by the word of the living God, which is quite rightly expected from the mouths of priests. For since nobody can be saved who has not first believed, it is the first task of priests as co-workers of the bishops to preach the Gospel of God to all. In this way they carry out the Lord's command, "Go into all the world and preach the Gospel to every creature" (Mk 16:15) and thus establish and increase the people of God.[17]

---

[16] *Catechism of the Catholic Church: Revised in Accordance with the Official Latin Text Promulgated by Pope John Paul II*. Vatican City: Libreria Editrice Vaticana, 1997.

[17] English translation available at: http://www.vatican.va/archive/hist _councils/ii_vatican_council/documents/vat-ii_decree_19651207 _presbyterorum-ordinis_en.html.

The article continues, stating that such actions lead to the beginning and growth (*incipit et crescit*) of the congregation of the faithful:

> For by the saving word of God faith is aroused in the heart of unbelievers and is nourished in the hearts of believers. By this faith then the congregation of the faithful begins and grows, according to the saying of the apostle: "Faith comes from what is heard, and what is heard comes by the preaching of Christ" (Rom 10:17).

The function of the priest also includes *bringing* the people to the worship of God (*ad Deum glorificandum eas adducunt*) through effective preaching that results in the application of the gospel truth in the everyday life of Christians:

> Priests owe it to everybody to share with them the truth of the Gospel in which they rejoice in the Lord. Therefore, whether by their exemplary behavior *they lead people to glorify God*; or by their preaching proclaim the mystery of Christ to unbelievers; or teach the Christian message or explain the Church's doctrine; or endeavor to treat of contemporary problems in the light of Christ's teaching—in every case their role is to teach not their own wisdom but the word of God and to issue a pressing invitation to all men and women to conversion and to holiness. Moreover, the priest's preaching, often very difficult in present-day conditions, if it is to become more effective in moving the minds of his hearers, must expound the word of God not merely in a general and abstract way but by an application of the eternal truth of the Gospel *to concrete circumstances of life.*[18]

The rest of article 4 acknowledges the many and varied ways by which the ministry of the word is carried out, ways that ultimately lead the laity to faith. It notes that this is especially true during

> the liturgy of the word within the celebration of Mass where there is an indivisible unity between the proclamation of the Lord's death and resurrection, the response of the hearers and the offering itself by which Christ confirmed the new covenant in his blood. In this offering the faithful share both by their prayer and by the reception of the sacrament.

[18] Emphasis added.

Article 5 follows and connects the functions of the priest with those of the bishop, both of whom are sharers in the priesthood of Christ in the performance of "sacred functions." These functions include the sacraments of baptism, penance, the anointing of the sick, and especially the celebration of the Mass. All of these sacraments, as well as all other ministries and apostolic works of the church, are directed toward the Eucharist:

> But the other sacraments, and indeed all ecclesiastical ministries and works of the apostolate are bound up [cohaerent] with the Eucharist and are directed toward it [ad eam ordinantur]. For in the most blessed Eucharist is contained the entire spiritual wealth of the Church [totum bonum spirituale Ecclesiae continetur], namely Christ himself our Pasch and our living bread, who gives life to people through his flesh—that flesh which is given life and gives life by the Holy Spirit. Thus people are invited and led to offer themselves, their works and all creation in union with Christ. *For this reason the Eucharist appears [apparet] as the source and summit [fons et culmen] of all preaching of the Gospel*: catechumens are gradually led forward to participation in the Eucharist, while the faithful who have already been consecrated in Baptism and Confirmation are fully incorporated in the body of Christ by the reception of the Eucharist.[19]

Coming at the end of the Second Vatican Council, article 5 of PO pulls together some of the components of both articles 10 and 12 of SC and article 11 of LG in its articulation of the Eucharist as source and summit. This section does not begin with the phrase containing "source and summit," as article 10 of SC had done, but instead, sets up the ecclesial context of church activities, followed by the relationship between Christ's presence and the Eucharist. It establishes the circumspective context of all church ministries (and here there is a direct link to article 9 of SC and its statement that *all* activities are *directed toward* the Eucharist). Then it states that *contained inside* the Eucharist is Christ himself, who is *the entire spiritual wealth of the church*. The *presence of Christ* within the Eucharist gives life to Christians so as to invite them to be laborers and join

---

[19] Emphasis added.

themselves to the offering of Christ. Given the focus of this entire document, there is a reference here to the sacrificial offering of the Mass. But even here there is a departure from article 7 of SC, which broke open the multiple ways in which Christ remains present in the eucharistic liturgy.

Since the entire document is focused on the nature, function, and spirituality of ordained priests, the Eucharist is named as source and summit, and not "the liturgy" *per se*, as articulated in article 10 of SC. Recall that in article 11 of LG the eucharistic *sacrifice* is the source and summit *of the Christian life* because *the faithful* offer the Divine Victim to God, and themselves along with him. PO's rearticulation of *why* the Eucharist is source and summit is more narrowly focused on the function of "the priesthood of the hierarchical ministry" (article 10 of LG). Thus by the end of the council these official statements as a whole not only reordered the Eucharist in relation to all other religious and spiritual practices but continued to maintain a clear preference for it by focusing on the clerical role that is involved in the performance of such practices.

The Writings of John Paul II and Benedict XVI

Part 3 of this chapter presents the writings of Popes John Paul II and Benedict XVI. John Paul II's writings on the Eucharist not only continue describing it as source and summit, and Sunday as the center of Christian life, but demonstrate a more dynamic interplay between the Eucharist and all other worship practices, particularly those that involve acts of social justice. First, I will present John Paul II's approach to articulating the Eucharist as source and summit and Sunday as the center of Christian life in his 1998 apostolic letter *The Lord's Day* and in his 2003 encyclical, *On the Eucharist in its Relationship to the Church*. Then I will demonstrate how John Paul II articulated the interrelationship between the Eucharist and the Christian activities of mercy, charity, and apostolic outreach. Finally I will summarize Benedict XVI's 2007 apostolic exhortation, *The Sacrament of Charity*, the most recent official statement on the Eucharist as source and summit.

John Paul II: Sunday as Center of Christian Life, and the Eucharist as
Source and Summit in Relation to Christian Practices of Social Justice

Pope John Paul II was a prolific writer throughout his entire pontificate (1978–2005). Worth noting here are two particular writings that continue the imagery of the Eucharist as source and summit, but also introduce a more explicit statement on Sunday as the center of Christian life: The Lord's Day (1998) and On the Eucharist in Its Relationship to the Church (2003).

In his 1998 apostolic letter, The Lord's Day (*Dies Domini*, hereafter DD), John Paul II responded to modern social practices and behaviors that are in tension with the Christian tradition of keeping Sunday as a holy day. Article 6 of the introduction states:

> Given this array of new situations and the questions which they prompt, it seems more necessary than ever *to recover the deep doctrinal foundations* underlying the Church's precept, so that the abiding value of Sunday in the Christian life will be clear to all the faithful. In doing this, we follow in the footsteps of the age-old tradition of the Church, powerfully restated by the Second Vatican Council in its teaching that on Sunday "Christian believers should come together, in order to commemorate the suffering, Resurrection and glory of the Lord Jesus, by hearing God's Word and sharing the Eucharist, and to give thanks to God who has given them new birth to a living hope through the Resurrection of Jesus Christ from the dead (cf. 1 Pt 1:3)."[20]

He connects the significance of Sunday to Christian duty in the next article and even suggests that Sunday is "the very heart of the Christian life":

> The duty to keep Sunday holy, especially by sharing in the Eucharist and by relaxing in a spirit of Christian joy and fraternity, is easily understood if we consider the many different aspects of this day upon which the present Letter will focus our attention.

[20] John Paul II, The Lord's Day, Apostolic Letter (Washington, DC: United States Catholic Conference, 1998), Introduction 6. Emphasis in original.

Sunday is a day which is at the very heart of the Christian life. From the beginning of my Pontificate, I have not ceased to repeat: "Do not be afraid! Open, open wide the doors to Christ!" In the same way, today I would strongly urge everyone to rediscover Sunday: *Do not be afraid to give your time to Christ!* Yes, let us open our time to Christ, that he may cast light upon it and give it direction. He is the One who knows the secret of time and the secret of eternity, and he gives us "his day" as an ever new gift of his love. The rediscovery of this day is a grace which we must implore, not only so that we may live the demands of faith to the full, but also so that we may respond concretely to the deepest human yearnings. Time given to Christ is never time lost, but is rather time gained, so that our relationships and indeed our whole life may become more profoundly human.[21]

Throughout the document, there are other references to summit and source or other comparable images. For example, in article 19, Easter is described as the source of the world's salvation;[22] in article 58 the Paschal Mystery is called the climax and source of Christian joy;[23] and in article 59 Christ is the culmination of the history of salvation.[24]

---

[21] Ibid., Introduction 7. Emphasis in original.

[22] DD, art. 19: "In the light of this constant and universal tradition, it is clear that, although the Lord's Day is rooted in the very work of creation and even more in the mystery of the biblical 'rest' of God, it is nonetheless to the Resurrection of Christ that we must look in order to understand fully the Lord's Day. *This is what the Christian Sunday does, leading the faithful each week to ponder and live the event of Easter, true source of the world's salvation.*" Emphasis supplied.

[23] DD, art. 58: "It is Christ, crucified and glorified, who comes among his disciples, to lead them all together into the newness of his Resurrection. *This is the climax, here below, of the covenant of love between God and his people: the sign and source of Christian joy, a stage on the way to the eternal feast.* This vision of faith shows the Christian Sunday to be a true 'time for celebration,' a day given by God to men and women for their full human and spiritual growth." Emphasis supplied.

[24] DD, art. 59: "More than a 'replacement' for the Sabbath, therefore, *Sunday is its fulfillment, and in a certain sense its extension and full expression in the ordered unfolding of the history of salvation, which reaches its culmination in Christ.*" Emphasis supplied.

In 2003, John Paul II wrote the encyclical On the Eucharist in Its Relationship to the Church (*Ecclesia de Eucharistia*, hereafter EE). Addressed to "The bishops, priests, and deacons, men and women in consecrated life, and all the lay faithful," the encyclical sought to articulate the relationship between the Eucharist and the church; indeed, its very title suggests that the church comes from/flows from the Eucharist. The very first article states:

> The Church draws her life from the Eucharist. This truth does not simply express a daily experience of faith, but recapitulates *the heart of the mystery of the Church*. In a variety of ways she joyfully experiences the constant fulfillment of the promise: "Lo, I am with you always, to the close of the age" (Mt 28:20), but in the Holy Eucharist, through the changing of bread and wine into the body and blood of the Lord, she rejoices in this presence with unique intensity. Ever since Pentecost, when the Church, the People of the New Covenant, began her pilgrim journey toward her heavenly homeland, the Divine Sacrament has continued to mark the passing of her days, filling them with confident hope.

Quoting article 11 of LG (and not SC), the article continues:

> The Second Vatican Council rightly proclaimed that the eucharistic sacrifice is "the source and summit of the Christian life." "For the most holy Eucharist contains the Church's entire spiritual wealth: Christ himself, our passover and living bread. Through his own flesh, now made living and life-giving by the Holy Spirit, he offers life to all." Consequently the gaze of the Church is constantly turned to her Lord, present in the Sacrament of the Altar, in which she discovers the full manifestation of his boundless love.

Striking in this section is the statement that the Eucharist contains "the Church's entire spiritual wealth" who is Christ himself, present in the bread. No reference is made to the wine.

In article 3, John Paul brings back the term "center" in its relation to the Eucharist and the life of the church: "The Church was born of the paschal mystery. For this very reason the Eucharist, which is in an outstanding way the sacrament of the paschal mystery, *stands at the center of the Church's life.*[25]

There are other places throughout the encyclical that use images of source and summit.[26] All of these articles are examples of how the term "the whole Christian life" casts a wide net of worship practices, from eucharistic adoration to Christian evangelization; it attempts to explain *what* liturgy does and how worship practices and activities flow *from* liturgy.

In addition, several of John Paul II's writings continue the vision of the early liturgical pioneers who maintained the interconnectedness between the Eucharist and Christian activities of social justice. Articles 69–72 of DD are devoted to this topic. Sunday Eucharist "commits [the faithful] even more 'to all the works of charity, of mercy, of apostolic outreach'" (art. 69). This connection between the Eucharist and social outreach may be traced back to apostolic times, since which "the Sunday gathering has in fact been for

---

[25] Emphasis in original.

[26] Article 10, Adoration of the Blessed Sacrament as Inexhaustible Source: "In many places, *adoration of the Blessed Sacrament* is also an important daily practice and becomes an inexhaustible source of holiness." (Emphasis in original.) Article 13, Eucharistic Sacrifice as Source and Summit (LG): "Taking part in the eucharistic Sacrifice, which is the source and summit of the whole Christian life, they offer the divine victim to God, and offer themselves along with it." Article 17, The Bread as the Source of Every Other Gift: "Through our communion in his body and blood, Christ also grants us his Spirit. Saint Ephrem writes: 'He called the bread his living body and he filled it with himself and his Spirit . . . He who eats it with faith, eats Fire and Spirit . . . Take and eat this, all of you, and eat with it the Holy Spirit. For it is truly my body and whoever eats it will have eternal life.' *The Church implores this divine Gift, the source of every other gift, in the eucharist epiclesis.* (Emphasis supplied.) Article 22, The Eucharist as Source and Summit of All Evangelization: "The eucharist thus appears as both the source and the summit of all evangelization, since its goal is the communion of humanity with Christ and in him with the Father and the Holy Spirit." Article 39, The Roman Pontiff as Source and Foundation of the Unity of the Bishops and the Faithful: "Likewise, since 'the Roman Pontiff, as the successor of Peter, is the perpetual and visible source and foundation of the unity of the Bishops and of the multitude of the faithful,' communion with him is intrinsically required for the celebration of the eucharistic Sacrifice."

Christians a moment of fraternal sharing with the poor," thus demanding a "culture of sharing, to be lived not only among the members of the community itself but also in society as a whole" (art. 70).[27] From the Eucharist "flows a tide of charity destined to spread into the whole life of the faithful, beginning by inspiring the very way in which they live the rest of Sunday" (art. 72). Indeed, the ebb and flow of these practices is not limited to what occurs *during* Sunday Eucharist but rather, as article 73 states,

> the whole of Sunday becomes a great school of charity, justice and peace. The presence of the Risen Lord in the midst of his people becomes an undertaking of solidarity, a compelling force for inner renewal, an inspiration to change the structures of sin in which individuals, communities and at times entire peoples are entangled.

Benedict XVI and The Sacrament of Charity

In more recent times Benedict XVI's 2007 post-synodal apostolic exhortation, The Sacrament of Charity (*Sacramentum Caritatis*, hereafter SOC), has a become the latest official statement on the

---

[27] In a particularly stirring quotation from St. John Chrysostom, art. 71 goes further and suggests that unless the hungry are fed, the vessels that are used during the Eucharist have no meaning: "Do you wish to honor the body of Christ? Do not ignore him when he is naked. Do you pay him homage in the temple clad in silk only then to neglect him outside where he suffers cold and nakedness[?] He who said: 'This is my body,' is the same One who said: 'You saw me hungry and you gave me no food,' and 'Whatever you did to the least of my brothers [and sisters] you did also to me.' What good is it if the eucharistic table is overloaded with golden chalices, when he is dying of hunger? Start by satisfying his hunger, and with what is left you may adorn the altar as well [Homilies on the Gospel of Matthew, 50.3-4].

A similar correlation of the integrity that is required between worship and acts of charity is found in John Paul II's address at the Great Mosque in Damascus, Syria, in 2001: "For all the times that Muslims and Christians have offended one another, we need to seek forgiveness from the Almighty and to offer each other forgiveness. . . . As members of the one human family and as believers, we have obligations to the common good, to justice and to solidarity. *Interreligious dialogue will lead to many forms of cooperation, especially in responding to the duty to care for the poor and the weak. These are the signs that our worship of God is genuine.*" (Emphasis supplied.)

Eucharist as "source and summit." Indeed, these very terms appear within its subtitle: "To the Bishops, Clergy, Consecrated Persons and the Lay Faithful on the Eucharist as the Source and Summit of the Church's Life and Mission."[28]

Not surprisingly, the terms "source" and "summit" appear throughout the document. But SOC goes deeper in articulating the relationship between the Eucharist and Christian life than what had been offered before. Its very subtitle, "The Eucharist as the Source and Summit of the Church's Life and Mission," suggests a particular focus on the eucharistic liturgy as distinct from all other types of liturgies. There is one section that moves through all seven sacraments (arts. 16–33), but even here it is only in reference to the eucharistic liturgy that attention is given to "source and summit." Also, the subtitle suggests a distinction between "the Church's life" and the "the Church's mission." The latter term "mission" is new in the sequence of official documents and denotes a more specific activity within the larger realm of "the Church's activity."

A significant passage is found within the introduction. In article 2 the location of "source" is found in the person of Jesus Christ:

> Each of us has an innate and irrepressible desire for ultimate and definitive truth. The Lord Jesus, "the way, and the truth, and the life" (Jn 14:6), speaks to our thirsting, pilgrim hearts, our hearts yearning for the source of life, our hearts longing for truth. Jesus Christ is the Truth in person, drawing the world to himself.[29]

That Jesus Christ is the source of the church's life is also found later, in article 34:

[28] The exhortation is a response to the proceedings, transcripts, and final report of the Eleventh Ordinary General Assembly of the Synod of Bishops, which met in Rome October 2–23, 2005. The Synod of Bishops was created by Paul VI on September 15, 1965, ten weeks before the close of the Second Vatican Council. These are international meetings by representative groups of bishops of the world who serve as advisors to the pope on a topic chosen by him.

[29] Benedict XVI, Post-Synodal Apostolic Exhortation, *Sacramentum Caritatis* (Washington, DC: United States Catholic Conference, 2007).

The Eucharist should be experienced as a mystery of faith, celebrated authentically and with a clear awareness that "the *intellectus fidei* has a primordial relationship to the Church's liturgical action." Theological reflection in this area can never prescind from the sacramental order instituted by Christ himself. On the other hand, the liturgical action can never be considered generically, prescinding from the mystery of faith. *Our faith and the eucharistic liturgy both have their source in the same event: Christ's gift of himself in the Paschal Mystery.*[30]

In this passage Christian faith in coupled with the Eucharist, both of which find their deeper source *in the event of Christ's sacrificial offering*.

Within the Introduction there is also a reintroduction of the term "center," which had previously appeared in the encyclicals of Pius XII:

In the sacrament of the Eucharist, Jesus shows us in particular the *truth about the love* which is the very essence of God. It is this evangelical truth which challenges each of us and our whole being. For this reason, the Church, which finds in the Eucharist the very center of her life, is constantly concerned to proclaim to all, *opportune importune* (cf. 2 Tim 4:2), that God is love. Precisely because Christ has become for us the food of truth, the Church turns to every man and woman, inviting them freely to accept God's gift.[31]

As noted above, SOC dedicates its entire third part (arts. 70–93) to the relationship between Eucharist and mission, but this is placed within a larger concern over the relationship between the Eucharist and Christian life. Entitled "The Eucharist, A Mystery to be Lived," this section develops the theme of a "eucharistic form of Christian life" that is further located within the larger category of "spiritual worship." Its two opening articles (70–71), have particular relevance to this book and thus deserve closer inspection,

[30] Emphasis supplied.
[31] Emphasis in original.

since it is within these two articles that Benedict XVI has reinterpreted article 10 of SC.

At the core to Benedict XVI's approach to understanding the Eucharist as source and summit is his application of Romans 12:1-2 and his interpretation of *logiké latreía* ("spiritual worship"), considered to be the turning point of the entire epistle: "I appeal to you therefore, brethren, by the mercies of God, to present your bodies as a living sacrifice, holy and acceptable to God, which is your spiritual worship. Do not be conformed to this world but be transformed by the renewal of your mind, that you may prove what is the will of God, what is good and acceptable and perfect." Thus it is in his interpretation of this Pauline notion of worship that we find Benedict XVI's attempt to relate the Eucharist to all other worship practices.

Article 70 begins with the assurance Jesus gave to his disciples: namely, that those who partake of his body and blood share in his promise of divine life.[32] Benedict then draws a connection between the Eucharist and "source and summit": "Here the eucharistic celebration appears in all its power as the source and summit of the Church's life, since it expresses at once both the origin and the fulfillment of the new and definitive worship of God, the *logiké*

---

[32] The first part of article 70 reads: "The Lord Jesus, who became for us the food of truth and love, speaks of the gift of his life and assures us that 'if any one eats of this bread, he will live for ever' (Jn 6:51). This 'eternal life' begins in us even now, thanks to the transformation effected in us by the gift of the Eucharist: 'He who eats me will live because of me' (Jn 6:57). These words of Jesus make us realize how the mystery 'believed' and 'celebrated' contains an innate power making it the principle of new life within us and the form of our Christian existence. By receiving the body and blood of Jesus Christ we become sharers in the divine life in an ever more adult and conscious way. Here too, we can apply Saint Augustine's words, in his *Confessions*, about the eternal Logos as the food of our souls. Stressing the mysterious nature of this food, Augustine imagines the Lord saying to him: 'I am the food of grown men; grow, and you shall feed upon me; nor shall you change me, like the food of your flesh, into yourself, but you shall be changed into me.' It is not the eucharistic food that is changed into us, but rather we who are mysteriously transformed by it. Christ nourishes us by uniting us to himself; 'he draws us into himself.' "

latreía." In his exegesis of Romans 12:1, Benedict connects the sacrifice of the Mass to the everyday sacrifice (offering) of Christian life, that is, *logiké latreía*, the entire living out of our whole lives in perfect worship of God:

> In these words the new worship appears as a total self-offering made in communion with the whole Church. The Apostle's insistence on the offering of our bodies emphasizes the concrete human reality of a worship which is anything but disincarnate. The Bishop of Hippo goes on to say that "this is the sacrifice of Christians: that we, though many, are one body in Christ. The Church celebrates this mystery in the sacrament of the altar, as the faithful know, and there she shows them clearly that in what is offered, she herself is offered."

Thus, as Christian doctrine has taught, "the Eucharist, as the sacrifice of Christ, is also the sacrifice of the Church, and thus of all the faithful."

A few observations are in order. First, Benedict XVI is placing the conversation with regard to source and summit within the larger scope of worship (specifically "spiritual worship"). He defines "spiritual worship" as "a total self-offering made in communion with the whole Church." Second, there is a further correspondence between Paul's understanding of "living sacrifice" and the eucharistic sacrifice that occurs on the altar, that is, the sacrifice of the church now united with the sacrifice of Christ on the cross as it is celebrated during the Eucharist. Third, to coordinate the juxtaposition of "sacrificial meaning" (and thus to justify his *reinterpretation* of Paul's approach to "spiritual worship"), Benedict uses writings from the tradition of the church, represented here by Augustine. Thus what makes "the eucharistic celebration" appear "in all its power as the source and summit of the Church's life" is that this celebration finds its origin (beginning) and fulfillment (end) in the *logiké latreía* that occurs in the sacrificial offering that unites the church to the sacrificial offering of Christ.

The result of our participation in the Eucharist (i.e., in "Christianity's new worship") is a transfiguration of Christian life, as the next article, 71, suggests:

Christianity's new worship includes and transfigures every aspect of life: "Whether you eat or drink, or whatever you do, do all to the glory of God" (1 Cor 10:31). Christians, in all their actions, are called to offer true worship to God. Here the intrinsically eucharistic nature of Christian life begins to take shape. The Eucharist, since it embraces the concrete, everyday existence of the believer, makes possible, day by day, the progressive transfiguration of all those called by grace to reflect the image of the Son of God (cf. Rom 8:29ff.).

Benedict XVI goes even further by promoting a more *exclusive* value of the Eucharist in the next line: "There is nothing authentically human—our thoughts and affections, our words and deeds—that does not find in the sacrament of the Eucharist the form it needs to be lived to the full." He ends this article by once again bringing the Eucharist within the larger context of the worship of God that occurs in the whole of Christian life:

> Here we can see the full human import of the radical newness brought by Christ in the Eucharist: the worship of God in our lives cannot be relegated to something private and individual, but tends by its nature to permeate every aspect of our existence. Worship pleasing to God thus becomes a new way of living our whole life, each particular moment of which is lifted up, since it is lived as part of a relationship with Christ and as an offering to God. The glory of God is humanity alive (cf. 1 Cor 10:31). And the human life is the vision of God.

Summary

In this third chapter I have presented the various rearticulations of the oft-cited terms "source" and "summit" and its accompanying phrases as they are found in official documents since the start of the Second Vatican Council, and have demonstrated that the uses of these terms in relation to the Eucharist coincided with the continuous strands that had developed during the liturgical movement, strands that sought to interrelate official liturgy, particularly the Eucharist, with all other non-official worship practices, including popular religion and acts of social justice. By the time the council sessions ended in 1965 the interpretive images of the Eucharist as source and summit of all other forms of worship became solidified, especially in article 10 of SC and article 11 of LG. This led to the promotion of this image, particularly in some of the post-conciliar statements by John Paul II and Benedict XVI.

As a result of solidifying and promoting the idea of the Eucharist as source and summit, less attention was given to articulating a genuine evaluation of popular religious practices in the everyday lives of Christians, at least within official documents. Popular religious practices were defined in relationship to—*in harmony and in accordance with*—official liturgy, while the Eucharist remained above all other worship practices, including the other sacraments. Further, as in the case of LG and PO, the promotion of the Eucharist as source and summit led to reflection on the role of the ordained priesthood, those who presided over the sacrifice of the Mass, to the detriment of any consideration of how the laity perform acts of non-official worship in their day-to-day lives.

But as post-conciliar reflections on the liturgical reforms emerged, as we have seen in some of the official statements by John Paul II and Benedict XVI, a more intentional consideration of interrelating the Eucharist with other forms of worship also began to emerge. John Paul II's statement of interplay between the Eucharist and acts of justice and charity provides a historical arch to the writings of Lambert Beauduin and Virgil Michel, while Benedict XVI's interpretation of *logiké latreía* placed the Eucharist in conversation with the larger worship of Christian life and activities.

Despite this ongoing dialectic between official and non-official worship practices, the paradigm of the Eucharist as source and summit remained, and we may well say it became even more deeply implanted within the minds of ecclesial leaders and liturgical scholars. In the next chapter I will turn to the discipline of liturgical theology and present some work by Peter Phan, who looks to the writings of Karl Rahner in order to propose a *quaestio disputata* with regard to the image of the Eucharist as source and summit while, at the same time, outlining another theological framework that considers the interplay between official liturgy and popular religion. I will also turn to other theologians such as

Robert J. Schreiter and Mark Francis in order to critique the terms "popular religion" and "popular piety" as these have been used thus far, so as to expand our concept of what constitute worship practices.

Chapter Four

The Liturgy of Life: The Interrelationship of Sunday Eucharist and Popular Devotions and the Extension of Worship Practices

Upon entering Helen Rosario's home one notices the dozens of pictures of saints taped to the walls and cabinets and displayed on her altars. The widowed Filipina, eighty-seven years old, has a dining-room altar filled with devotional pictures, rosaries, pendants, a few candles, and prayer cards. "I really love to pray!" she immediately informs me. "Well, most of the time when I have nothing to do, I pray." Her "bedroom altar," which is even larger, is located right across from her bed.[1] Displayed are fifty-five devotional pictures of saints, five different-sized statues of saints, a crucifix positioned at the top center, and another cross made out of a palm branch. Her dining-room altar is situated on top of a cabinet and includes two large bouquets of silk flowers, one small vase containing fresh flowers, three large statues (the Sacred Heart of Jesus, the Holy Family, and Our Lady of Guadalupe), a candle stand, a rosary, a dozen medallions, and some prayer booklets . . . and this description does not include her "third altar" in the foyer, and her kitchen cabinets, bathroom, and walls. The dozens of religious and devotional objects mirror her everyday prayer life in which every hour is accounted for, from 7:00 AM to 11:00 PM.[2] This includes the recitation of devotional prayers, daily Mass at St. Agnes at 8:30 AM,

---

[1] See appendix 3, p. 181.
[2] See appendix 4, p. 183.

and eucharistic adoration every Tuesday morning for one hour. But of all the prayers she regularly prays, the Angelus is her favorite.

After we sat down for an interview at her dining-room table I asked her to describe her prayer life.

Ricky: Why is the Angelus your favorite?

Helen: Well, because I grew up with my grandmother. Every time she says those prayers. I don't understand what it means, but I got it for my grandmother. [*She smiles and starts reciting the whole prayer in Latin.*]
You see? From my grandma! I memorized it!

Ricky: So it reminds you of your grandmother whenever you recite it.

Helen: Oh yes! Well, because we grew up with her. I was sixteen when my mother died. And I was nineteen [when] my father died. Because my father was a schoolteacher, we had a good life. And then, when they are gone, no more. So it was very tough.

Ricky: How would you compare the Angelus with Mass? Is there a relationship between the two or no?

Helen: Well, I believe that the Mass is honoring God, first of all, and then, also, to ask forgiveness of my sins. That's how I feel. And I know that the priest guides us, like the readings of the gospel. I don't have all the time to search for the gospel, but in the Mass he reminds us what is the theme for today. So I love to go to Mass. I believe that there's spirituality.

Ricky: What do you mean by spirituality?

Helen: I mean to say that God will help in all your needs and the life after. We're like making an investment for heaven. That's how I feel.

Later, I ask her to compare her favorite prayer with the daily Mass.

Ricky: So how would you compare praying the Angelus with going to daily Mass?

Helen: They are all the same to me, meaning to say that God is listening to what I'm asking for . . . for pardon of my sins especially.

Ricky: Are you saying that God doesn't listen to you more during the Mass than He does during the Angelus?

Helen: Yes, it's all the same. That's how I feel, because God does not discriminate. He does not say, "Oh, your prayer is not good." No, He does not do that! [*She laughs and continues to provide me with a list of others prayers she recites.*]

Ricky: It sounds like every hour and every moment of your life is prayer to God.

Helen: Oh sure.

Ricky: And because it's prayer to God and God listens to all our prayers, then there is no discrimination between Sunday Mass, the Angelus, rosaries, and prayers to St. Anthony.

Helen: I believe that God is always listening because God does not discriminate. I'm just a human being only; God is perfect.

At my second interview with Helen, I asked: "Who or What is the source of your life?" She gave me a one-word answer, "God," and then added: "Because God really loves me and gives all these things to me . . . [otherwise] He should not have created me. But because He loves me so much, He created me. See? That's my belief!"

❖　❖　❖

For Edward, regular attendance at AA meetings led to his encounter with a Jesuit priest who recommended that he visit St. Agnes. He had been searching for "some kind of community . . . something bigger." Edward eventually found the "connection" (his term) he had lost, primarily through the "fellowship and community" he experienced at St. Agnes. At one point he disrupted my line of questioning, which, in hindsight, made me acutely aware of how I prejudged my ethnographic participants during the interviewing process: "You keep asking me about what I think about 'the Mass.' I don't come here on Sunday for the *Mass*; I come here because of this *community*, the *fellowship* with one another." For Edward, both AA meetings and the "community of St. Agnes" "re-connect" him with "the higher power!" AA spirituality "is the *same* spirituality as the Mass," but during AA meetings "there is a deeper fellowship and trust among us." Choosing to go to St. Agnes was "the second best decision [he] made for [him]self," but [his] "first best decision was going to AA."

❖   ❖   ❖

The ethnographic interviews I conducted helped me to rethink the popular use of the statement: "the Eucharist is the source and summit of Christian life." A number of theological books and articles have referenced article 10 of SC or article 11 of LG. Most of these resources used the various terms and phrases from these articles and even nuanced their meanings in order to promote the spirit and pastoral objectives of the council. For example, there are two books that actually bear these terms in their titles: Adolf Adam's *The Eucharistic Celebration: The Source and Summit of Faith* (1994)[3] is not a theological presentation on the meaning of "source and summit" but more of a pastoral commentary on the 1975 *General Instruction on the Roman Missal*. In 1999 a *Festschrift* was dedicated to Josef Jungmann; its title is *Source and Summit: Commemorating Josef A. Jungmann, S.J.*[4] These terms were included within the general title of the book in order to group together a number of theological perspectives on the liturgy.[5] To this extent "the liturgy as source and summit" has continued to serve as a generalizing metaphor for theological reflections on the official

[3] Adolf Adam, *The Eucharistic Celebration: The Source and Summit of Faith*, trans. Robert C. Schultz (Collegeville, MN: Liturgical Press, 1994).

[4] Joanne M. Pierce and Michael Downey, eds., *Source and Summit: Commemorating Josef A. Jungmann, S.J.* (Collegeville, MN: Liturgical Press, 1999).

[5] These include, among others, Kathleen Hughes, Gerard Austin, John Baldovin, John Melloh, Peter Fink, Don Saliers, Monica Hellwig, and Regis Duffy.

82

worship practices of the church, usually with a primary focus on the Eucharistic liturgy.

Likewise, some articles in theological journals have made use of these terms but, unlike the books mentioned above, these articles found new ways of applying their popular use. In his 1983 article, "Worship: The Source and Summit of Faith,"[6] Philip Pfatteicher transported the terms into his own Lutheran tradition, thus confirming their ecumenical significance. In 1990, James O'Connor placed the terms in conversation with social justice, thus adding to the growing list of Gospel values that flow from the liturgy.[7] He also continued the insights begun by some of the early liturgical pioneers, including Lambert Beauduin and Virgil Michel. By 1995 it was more than clear that the statement "the liturgy is the source and summit of Christian life" had become, in the words of Arno Schilson, a "programmatic conciliar phrase."[8]

More recently the Benedictine theologian Jeremy Driscoll championed liturgy as the source and summit of Christian life by providing a more detailed reflection on how this phrase relates to *logiké latreía* in Romans 12:1-2.[9] In his 2009 article, "Worship in the Spirit of Logos: Romans 12:1-2 and the Source and Summit of Christian Life," Driscoll in many ways develops the content of articles 70 and 71 of Benedict XVI's SOC. He provides, first, an

[6] Philip Pfatteicher, "Worship: The Source and Summit of Faith," *Consensus* 9/2 (1983): 13–25.

[7] James T. O'Connor, "The Eucharist: Source and Summit of Justice and Charity," *Social Justice Review* 81 (Nov–Dec. 1990): 197–99.

[8] Arno Schilson, "Liturgy as 'Summit and Source' of Christian Life: Origin and Meaning of a Programmatic Conciliar Phrase," *Living Light* 31 (Spring 1995): 57–67.

[9] "I appeal to you therefore, brethren, by the mercies of God, to present your bodies as a living sacrifice, holy and acceptable to God, which is your spiritual worship. Do not be conformed to this world but be transformed by the renewal of your mind, that you may prove what is the will of God, what is good and acceptable and perfect" (Rom 12:1-2). Translation in Jeremy Driscoll, "Worship in the Spirit of Logos: Romans 12:1-2 and the Source and Summit of Christian Life," *Letter & Spirit* 5 (2009): 77–101, at 80. Driscoll's translation of Romans 12:1-2 is drawn from both the Revised Standard Version [RSV] and New American Bible [NAB].

exegetical exposition of Romans 12:1-2, and second, a "liturgical realization" of the text, "that is, not so much what [these verses] may have meant in the immediate context in which Paul was writing, but their meaning after two millennia of the Church's meditation upon them and their application to the liturgy."[10]

The idea that the liturgy is the source and summit of church life has not been accepted without criticism. In "Liturgy of Life as the 'Summit and Source' of the Eucharistic Liturgy: Church Worship as Symbolization of the Liturgy of Life?,"[11] Peter Phan challenges this theological trajectory by raising "a genuine *quaestio disputata*"[12] regarding the relationship between worship and life. He questions the meaning of the oft-cited phrase in article 10 of SC, "The liturgy is the summit toward which the activity of the Church is directed; it is also the fount from which all her power flows," and proposes a theological hypothesis that not only challenges SC's assertion but positions "the liturgy of life [as] the 'summit and source' of the eucharistic liturgy and not the other way around."[13]

In this chapter I will first provide some background to the resistance to article 10 of SC during the Second Vatican Council. I will devote the next section to Phan's insight and explanation of the liturgy of life. Phan primarily focuses on popular religion as an

---

[10] Ibid., 77.

[11] Peter C. Phan, "Liturgy of Life as Summit and Source of Eucharistic Liturgy: Church Worship as Symbolization of the Liturgy of Life?" 257–78 in idem, *Being Religious Interreligiously: Asian Perspectives on Interfaith Dialogue in Postmodernity* (Maryknoll, NY: Orbis Books, 2004).

[12] *Quaestio disputata* ("disputed question"; plural: *quaestiones disputatae*) was a formal scholastic method that traces back to the early twelfth century in Europe; it declined in popularity by the eighteenth. This style and format of questions and responses arose in the context of lectures delivered in medieval universities in which the lecturer (the *magister*) would have to defend his thesis by answering the objections raised by a *baccalaureus respondens* (formally appointed by the presiding master) who represented both the students and other faculty members of the university. According to Brian Lawn, the goal of these formal disputations was not only to challenge the master but also to test the skills of the students. See his *The Rise and Decline of the Scholastic* Quaestio Disputata (Leiden: Brill, 1993).

[13] Phan, "Liturgy of Life," 257.

example of non-official worship. To extend his proposal and consider how *all* worship practices may be placed in conversation with official liturgy, I will then demonstrate some problematic uses of the terms "popular religion" and "popular piety," and present Robert Schreiter's proposal for how theological method may include three considerations that extend the worship boundaries beyond popular religion and official liturgy.

Resistance and Debate over Article 10 of the Constitution on the Sacred Liturgy

Josef Jungmann provides some detailed commentary on the resistance to the approval of article 10 of SC by the Central Commission during their deliberations. At the start, council participants had to elucidate the relationship between "the liturgy" and "Church life":

> This elucidation was recognized to be necessary in view of exaggerated assessments of the liturgy on the one hand, as if they were identical with the life of the Church, and on the other hand, in view of activistic misunderstanding, which intended to ascribe to it only a marginal function beside the accomplishments of apostolate, preaching, mission and organization.[14]

The preparatory commission balanced these two poles by (1) naming the specific "extra-liturgical activities" that move unbelievers toward becoming "living members of the Church" (article 9), and (2) providing a more "positive statement"[15] asserting that the liturgy is the summit and fount of all activities of the church.

Despite the attempts by the preparatory commission to seek balance between these two poles through their careful wording of article 10, misgivings were raised through a series of proposed amendments during the final voting:

[14] Josef Andreas Jungmann, "Constitution on the Sacred Liturgy," in *Commentary on the Documents of Vatican II*, vol. 1, ed. Herbert Vorgrimler (New York: Herder and Herder, 1967), 15.

[15] Ibid.

In the text which came from the Central Commission and was placed before the Council the sentence had been modified. Yet, according to it, the liturgy is "in its center, that is, in the divine sacrifice of the Eucharist," the summit and fountain. But in spite of this new version, misgivings about the sentence were expressed in the assembly: in the view of the opponents one could not say even of the Eucharist that everything without exception was ordered in relation to it and proceeded from it.[16]

Jungmann names four points of resistance that emerged among council members:

The summit and goal of the activity of the church [was not the liturgy, but] . . . the salvation of souls and the glory of God;

the highest virtue was not religion, but love;

the liturgy was rather a means than an end, the fountain being Christ and the Holy Ghost;

the liturgy [as it was presented in this article] appeared here in a sense only very meagerly explained.[17]

As a counter to these points, Jungmann refers to the context of the article and argues:

[T]he statement was not a judgment on religious values in general, but pertained merely to the total efficacy of the church in the world and the many sided ramification of her pastoral care. All this work must in fact find its outlet in worship and again and again receive stimulus and right orientation from it. The schema named only the praise of God and the Lord's Supper.

Eventually a modification was made to include the church's participation in the sacrifice of the Mass ("to take part in the Sacrifice"). But in the end it was through the insistence of Bishop Henri Jenny,

[16] Ibid.
[17] Ibid.

a consultor to the preparatory commission, that the original text with its "comprehensive statement" was maintained. "The Council Commission gave him its approval and the article was accepted by the Council in its original form by 2004 votes to 101."[18]

Peter Phan and the Liturgy of Life as Summit and Source

Critiquing the Church's Liturgy as Summit and Source

Systematic theologian Peter Phan offers a theological paradigm that does not limit the contextual horizon of liturgical scholarship to eucharistic liturgies alone but, instead, broadens the scope and spectrum of what constitutes "liturgy" by borrowing Karl Rahner's "liturgy of the world" and renaming it "the liturgy of life." Further, Phan proposes that the liturgy of life is the summit and source of the official liturgy and popular religion and that *both* of these worship practices together constitute the one worship that humanity renders to God.

Phan divides his proposal into three parts: (1) a history of Vatican II's teaching on article 10 of SC, including "possible theological misinterpretations and pastoral misapplications" of the article; (2) a theological foundation for his thesis based on the writings of Karl Rahner; and (3) an exploration of the nature and function of popular religion in relation to the Eucharist and within the larger framework of the liturgy of life.[19]

Phan notes the objections and proposed amendments regarding the wording of article 10 of SC (see above). Despite these objections, Phan acknowledges that the use of the metaphors *culmen* (summit) and *fons* (fount) in article 10 may be theologically justified for two reasons. First, article 7 of SC states that the liturgy is "an exercise of the priestly office of Jesus Christ . . . and of His Body which is the Church . . . a sacred action *surpassing all others*" (emphasis added). If this is so, Phan asks, "in what sense is the liturgy the summit toward which the activities of the church are directed? Is it in the

[18] Ibid.
[19] Phan, "Liturgy of Life," 257.

sense that the liturgy constitutes the end of the church's life?"[20] Phan's careful reading of the last sentence of article 10 reveals that the activities of the church are directed toward the sanctification of humanity and the glorification of God "as toward their end." Thus the liturgy should only be viewed "indirectly" as the summit of church activities.

The second theological argument for the inclusion of these metaphors has to do with the liturgy's efficacy, since "[n]o other action of the church is said to equal that efficacy 'by the same title and to the same degree.'" But here Phan points out that this efficacy is by way of *ex opere operato* [by the work having been performed] and not *ex opere operantis* [by the work of the agent]. "The supreme excellence of the Eucharist, then, lies in the special presence of Christ 'in the eucharistic species' (SC, no. 7),"[21] as long as this is understood to be in relationship with the other modes of Christ's presence, as stated in SC 7: Christ is present in the minister, in the word of God, and in the assembly.

Theological Interpretations and Pastoral Applications

Have the various mantras and usages of the term "source and summit" unintentionally resulted in a misunderstanding or misappropriation of these terms? To what degree have we used (or even exaggerated) article 10 without taking into account its qualifying and surrounding articles, such as, "The liturgy *does not exhaust the entire activity* of the Church" (article 9, emphasis added), or "From the liturgy, therefore, particularly the Eucharist, grace is poured forth upon us as from a fountain; the liturgy is the source for achieving in the most effective way possible human sanctification and God's glorification, *the end to which all the Church's other activities are directed*" (article 10, emphasis added)?

It is not Phan's goal to diminish the importance or centrality of the eucharistic liturgy in the life of the church: "On the pastoral side, Sunday Masses are the focal point around which the life of the parish revolves . . . the gathering point of the parish commu-

---

[20] Ibid., 260.
[21] Ibid.

nity."[22] But while the doctrine that the liturgy is the summit and source of church life may be theologically justified, he asks whether this has led to "one-sided theological interpretations and skewed pastoral practices."[23]

First, the image of "summit" suggests "a mountain or a pyramid," a medieval paradigm that

> emphasizes fixed order, teleology, substance, hierarchy, anthropocentrism, dualism and kingdom in contrast to the postmodern paradigm, which stresses evolution and historical emergence, structure and openness, mutual relation and interdependence, systems and wholes, organicism, multileveled composition, and community . . . sets up a scale of values and willy-nilly devalues all other activities, ecclesial or otherwise, that do not qualify as liturgical or sacramental.[24]

Phan asks whether there is another metaphor "that fosters fundamental equality, mutual relationship, reciprocal dependence, openness, change, and novelty in the way the liturgy and the Eucharist interact with other activities of the church."[25]

Second, the metaphor *fons* suggests a "one-way relation between the original source and the body of water that flows out of it . . . from the top to the bottom." This image systematically excludes "any possibility of fecundation and enrichment of the liturgy and the Eucharist by other forms of worship or sacramental celebration, let alone popular devotions and daily life in general."[26]

Third, the two metaphors support a post-Tridentine theology that views Christians as living in two different and separate worlds, the secular and the sacred. The larger world of everyday life, the world of Monday through Saturday and even the greater part of Sunday,

---

[22] Ibid., 261.

[23] Ibid.

[24] Ibid., 261–62. Phan refers to Ian Barbour, *Religion in an Age of Science* (New York: Harper & Row, 1979), 219.

[25] Phan, "Liturgy of Life," 262.

[26] Ibid.

is secular and devoid of grace because it is only "nature" and worse, fallen and sinful.[27]

The Liturgy of Life as Everyday Mystical Encounters with God

In response to these interpretations and pastoral practices, Phan offers another metaphor and widen the liturgical horizon beyond Sunday Mass in order to account for the everyday generative experiences and worship practices through which Christians encounter God. He draws inspiration from the theological writings of Karl Rahner,[28] in which *the entire world* is viewed as being wholly permeated by God's grace: "Strictly speaking, therefore, there are not secular and sacred zones in human history, no profane marketplace and holy temple, but only the saved (where God's self-gift is accepted) and the damned (where it is rejected)."[29]

Because of the permeation of the world by God's grace, Christians are called to be "mystics" in the world, that is, to be *attuned* to the presence of God during everyday moments that would otherwise go unnoticed.[30] Experiences of God are not rare but are avail-

---

[27] Ibid., 262–63.

[28] As "an outline of Rahner's most important theological reflections in support of [his] position," Phan cites "two most important essays" by Rahner: "Considerations on the Active Role of the Person in the Sacramental Event," *Theological Investigations* 14 (New York: Seabury, 1976), 161–84; and "On the Theology of Worship," *Theological Investigations* 19 (New York: Crossroad, 1983), 141–49. He also recommends Michael Skelley, *The Liturgy of the World: Karl Rahner's Theology of Worship* (Collegeville, MN: Liturgical Press, 1991).

[29] Phan, "Liturgy of Life," 267.

[30] Michael Skelley describes Rahner's concept of mysticism: "The heart of the mystical experience is the experience of the absolute mystery of God. That experience can take place with or without the extraordinary phenomena usually associated with mysticism. Mysticism is conventionally identified with unusual psychophysical phenomena such as visions, locutions, ecstasies, dreams and trances . . . . Within this understanding of mysticism, mystics are a very elite group, and their experience of God is not something we would expect to share. But Rahner argues that the psychophysical phenomena usually identified with mysticism are secondary gifts that are only sometimes given with the greater gift of the experience of God. The secondary gifts should not be confused with the primary gift. Experience of God is in fact normally offered to us without any of these ancillary gifts." *The Liturgy of the World*, 76–77.

able to everyone at all places and at all times. Where Rahner calls these mystical encounters with God "the liturgy of the world"/ "the Mass of the world," Phan, for his part, encapsulates these terms in his own, "the liturgy of life." This includes the "universal experiences of God and mystical encounters with God's grace in the midst of everyday life, made possible by God's self-gift embracing the whole human history, always and everywhere."[31] In addition to stating that the liturgy of life is made available to us in the midst of everyday life by God, and that it is "necessarily diffuse [and] unstructured" and hence "easily [goes] unnoticed," Phan notes that the liturgy of life has a christological character since "Jesus' sacrifice on the cross" (Jesus' liturgy) "derived its origin or emerged from" the liturgy of life.[32] That is to say, the event of Jesus' liturgy (from his incarnation to his passion, death, and resurrection) is forever and intimately connected to God's continued self-communication to the world. The liturgy of life, in turn, encompasses our "Christ-response" of worship to God's gracious self-communication in history.[33]

Finally, Phan proposes that the liturgy of life "is the very source of fecundity and effectiveness of the liturgy of the church," since "humanity's ongoing communion with God in grace in daily life is, according to Rahner, the primary and original liturgy." The worship of God, then, involves those explicit moments when Christians celebrate these encounters, made even more explicit during the church's official *public* liturgies. But the aforementioned "one-sided theological interpretations and skewed pastoral practices" may result if Christians do not acknowledge that official liturgies take place within the wider horizon of these everyday mystical encounters.[34]

---

[31] Phan, "Liturgy of Life," 268–69.

[32] Ibid., 270.

[33] As Phan explains: "the incarnation, death, and resurrection of the Logos brought it [the liturgy of life] to its fullest fulfillment and constitutes its supreme point. Through these events God's self-communication in history became definitive, irrevocable, irreversible, insofar as it is now both *offer* and *acceptance* indissolubly united as one in the person of Jesus." Ibid.

[34] Ibid., 271.

Church Liturgy as "Real Symbol" of the Liturgy of Life

Using Rahner's theology of the symbol, Phan articulates the relationship between the liturgy of life and the liturgy of the church, that is, "the liturgy of the church is the 'real symbol' of the liturgy of life."[35] A symbol is " 'the reality, constituted by the thing symbolized as an inner moment of itself, which reveals and proclaims the thing symbolized, and is itself full of the thing symbolized, being its concrete form of existence.' "[36] Phan then lists five theological and pastoral implications. "First, as the thing symbolized and its symbol constitute an ontological and indissoluble unity, so the liturgy of life and the liturgy of the church constitute the one worship that humanity renders to God and whose center and supreme fulfillment is Jesus Christ."[37] Second, the liturgy of life becomes "real, present, and effective in the liturgy of the church" through the "explicit rituals and prayers of the church worship and sacraments." Third, the liturgy of the church, in turn, "does not exist by itself and is not effective except as a symbolization of the liturgy of life."[38] The liturgy of the church makes the liturgy of life "concretely present here and now in the consciousness of the faithful." Fourth, the relationship between the liturgy of life and the liturgy of the church is marked by "a dynamic, two-way, mutual interdependence." They are "two intrinsic dimensions of the one reality, correcting and enriching each other."[39] Since the liturgy of life is "more original and more fundamental," it is the summit and source of the liturgy of the church. At the same time, Phan qualifies this by stating that the summit, center, and source of both the liturgy of life *and* the liturgy of the church is "Jesus Christ, who in his incarnation, ministry, death, and resurrection brought God's self-communication to the world to its irrevocable, irreversible,

[35] Ibid., 272.

[36] Karl Rahner, "The Theology of the Symbol," 221–51 in *Theological Investigations* 4 (Baltimore: Helicon, 1966), 251. Quoted in Phan, "Liturgy of Life," 271–72.

[37] Phan, "Liturgy of Life," 272.

[38] Ibid.

[39] Ibid., 273.

and victorious fulfillment."[40] Finally, in addressing the quality of effectiveness, Phan states that one does not bring the other into existence: "Rather, there is between them a relation of formal or 'symbolic' causality by which the one comes into being either by being symbolized by the other or by being the symbol of the other, that is, by the self-expression of the other in this symbol."[41]

Interrelating the Liturgy of the Church and Popular Religion within the Liturgy of Life

By demonstrating how the liturgy of life is the source and summit of the liturgy of the church, Phan essentially sets up a dialectical paradigm between the liturgy of the church and all other forms of worship activities. Thus, in the concluding section of his chapter Phan considers the place of popular religion within his schema and proposes that, in addition to the liturgy of the church, popular religion may also be viewed as a real symbol of the liturgy of life.

The reason he chooses to highlight popular religion is the state of popular religious practices since the Second Vatican Council. At one level there has been a noticeable resurgence of popular religious practices throughout the world. At another level, this is due "to the widespread dissatisfaction with the classical form of Vatican II's reformed rites characterized by Roman *sobrietas*, *brevitas*, *simplicitas*, and linear rationality, which do not respond to the people's need for emotional and total involvement in liturgical celebrations."[42]

Arguing that popular religion has often been placed in a subservient role in relationship to the liturgy of the church, at least in official documents, Phan places popular religion in a more intentional and mutual dialogue with the liturgy of life. The key theological linkage between popular religion and the liturgy of the church is developed in his exposition of symbolization, something he had outlined earlier: "I suggest we view [popular religion] as

[40] Ibid.
[41] Ibid.
[42] Ibid., 275.

the symbolization of the liturgy of life, a symbolization that is parallel to the symbolization of the liturgy of life by the church liturgy, and therefore needs to be assessed on its own terms and not in dependence on the church liturgy."[43] He then defends the way this new paradigm for interrelating popular religion and the liturgy of the church places both of these worship practices in alignment with one another while maintaining their distinctiveness. Thus, as "symbol of the liturgy of life, popular religion is related to it in very much the same way as the church liturgy is related to it"; both the liturgy of the church *and* popular religion are real symbols of the liturgy of life. Collectively, these mystical encounters with God's grace in the world create a dynamic and mutual interdependency that points toward the unity of the one worship of God through Christ and in the power of the Holy Spirit:

> In brief, the liturgy of life and popular religion form the one worship rendered to God, though each retains its distinctive identity. The liturgy of life becomes real, effective, and concrete in and through popular religion, just as popular religion achieves its effectiveness by being the real symbol of the liturgy of life. Between them there is a mutual causal relationship characterized not by efficient causality but by formal or symbolic causality.[44]

The Search for Adequate Terms for Considering the Scope and Spectrum of Worship Practices

Phan's use of the term "popular religion" or "popular religiosity" (*religiosidad popular*) demonstrates the difficulty and limitations of worship terminology that attempts to take into account the interrelationship of these practices with official liturgy. As we saw earlier, article 13 of SC uses the term "popular devotions" (*pia exercitia*), which Phan acknowledges in his reference to Domenico Sartore's fourfold classification of popular devotions:

[43] Ibid., 276.
[44] Ibid., 277.

First, devotions to Christ, the Blessed Virgin, and the saints in the forms of pilgrimages, patronal feasts, processions, popular devotions, and novenas; second, the rites related to the liturgical year; third, traditional practices in conjunction with the celebrations of the sacraments and other Christian rites like funerals; and fourth, institutions and religious objects connected with various forms of popular religiosity.[45]

But to what extent do the terms "popular religion" and "popular devotions" take into account the scope and spectrum of all forms of worship practices? In *Constructing Local Theologies* (a work from which Phan borrows heavily in his last section on popular religion), Robert Schreiter breaks open the complexity of the term "popular religion" and places it alongside two other terms, "folk religion," and "common religion."[46] While "all three of these terms have their specific strengths and weaknesses," Schreiter contends, "[p]opular religion" remains "the most common of the terms," even though it "lacks a certain specificity."[47] He thus chooses to use this term for the duration of his presentation on the construction of a local theology that takes popular religious practices into consideration. (This may also explain Phan's use of the term "popular religion.") With reference to Schreiter, Phan writes: "Whether under the rubric of popular religion, or folk religion, or common religion, it is well known that nonliturgical, non-official, popular expressions of religiosity (popular not in the sense of

[45] See ibid., 275, citing Anscar Chupungco, *Liturgical Inculturation: Sacramentals, Religiosity, and Catechesis* (Collegeville, MN: Liturgical Press, 1992), 102, summarizing Domenico Sartore, "Le manifestazione della religiosità popolare," *Anamnesis* 7 (Genoa, 1989): 232–33.

[46] Robert J. Schreiter, *Constructing Local Theologies* (Maryknoll, NY: Orbis Books, 1985), 124–43.

[47] Ibid., 124–25. Concerning the strengths and weaknesses of folk and common religion, he writes: " 'Folk' has the specificity, but carries strong (and often negative) overtones. 'Common' has a sense similar to 'popular' and is in some ways the most useful term, but it is also the least well known." Ibid., 125.

'in fashion' but in the sense of 'the people in general') received scant attention from Vatican II."[48]

The 2001 *Directory on Popular Piety and the Liturgy*,[49] which was issued by the Congregation for Divine Worship and the Discipline of the Sacraments, places "popular religiosity" alongside "popular piety" but admits that these lack "a uniform terminology."[50] The directory, nevertheless, goes on to define the "commonly understood" terms, "pious exercise," "devotions," "popular piety," and "popular religiosity" (arts. 7–10). Many of the contributors to the *Directory on Popular Piety and the Liturgy: A Commentary* (edited by Phan), expressed criticism of the document's attempt to create such categories; for example, Mark Francis writes:

> Despite the attempts of the directory to clarify such expressions . . . the historical reality that underlies these terms is much more messy than the definitions seem to suggest. These categories are defined by the directory in terms of their distance or closeness to the liturgy. . . . These definitions only approximate the reality they describe, since they are largely derived from a nineteenth-century European understanding of what constitutes popular piety. In reality, there is much more overlap between "popular piety" and "popular religion."[51]

Moreover, as James Empereur points out, the document's attempt to interrelate popular religion and official liturgy is not any more successful:

> Throughout the directory there is an ambiguity about the relationship of the liturgy to popular piety. On the one hand, it wants to draw clear-cut lines between the two, and on the other, when it refers to concrete practices, it is not always clear if it is talking about

[48] Phan, "Liturgy of Life," 274.

[49] Congregation for Divine Worship and the Discipline of the Sacraments, Directory on Popular Piety and the Liturgy: Principles and Guidelines (Vatican City: Libreria editrice Vaticana, 2001).

[50] Ibid., article 6.

[51] Francis, "Liturgy and Popular Piety in a Historical Perspective," 19–44 in *Directory on Popular Piety and the Liturgy: Principles and Guidelines: A Commentary*, at 26–27.

the liturgy as such or some amplification of it that does not qualify as popular piety. It has been pointed out that despite the official insistence on the primacy of Sunday, it has been modified by such exceptions as Divine Mercy Sunday and the permission to substitute the celebration of our Lady of Guadalupe when it falls on a Sunday. Perhaps this is a recognition that it is not always possible to draw such clear parameters around those areas affected by liturgical legislation.[52]

These observations align with Schreiter's remarks about the three relational contrasts that have developed in popular religious practices. Mindful that the term "popular" remains the common link between these two terms, Schreiter observes that popular religion is sometimes contrasted with official religion, with "elite religion," and by a contrast between the "esoteric" and the "exoteric":

> These three contrasting uses of "popular" bespeak three different axes along which popular religion is interpreted: institutional, social, and intellectual. While certainly not totally discrete categories, they represent distinctive conceptions of the major role of religion in society: as one of institutional organization, of social formation, of intellectual achievement.[53]

Given these relational contrasts, Schreiter proposes three considerations in the construction of a theological method that takes seriously the place of popular religion. These considerations have implications for the goals of this book. First, Schreiter states that concern over popular religion "seems to arise from the side of official and elite groups." In this light, several questions may be asked: for example, for whom is popular religion an issue and why is it an issue for them? and "does an elitist group see it as an inferior product of the culture, which needs to be brought into the mainstream of 'progress'?"[54] The obvious implication here is that the

---

[52] James Empereur, "Popular Piety and the Liturgy: Principles and Guidelines," 1–18 in *Directory on Popular Piety and the Liturgy: Principles and Guidelines: A Commentary*, at 10.

[53] *Constructing Local Theologies*, 125.

[54] Ibid., 126.

study of popular religion needs to consider more intentionally the opinions, experiences, and practices that arise from the people themselves, that is, from the non-official, the nonelite, or (as I will show in the next chapter) the nonexperts.

Second, "religion seems to be construed here as a set of ideas, which then shape a particular practice."[55] Popular religion is a Western and intellectual bias, whereas for "the greater part of the world" religion is more a way of life than a view of life. In other words, approaches that first name religious ideas and then attempt to derive practices that emerge from those ideas are likened to putting "the cart before the horse." The implications here may be applied to the call to study the *lived practices* of popular religion rather than limit the study of religion to texts and doctrinal statements alone. How do living and breathing humans ritually engage in worship, and how do these practices, in turn, align or not align with theological, official, or doctrinal discourses on such practices?

Third, Schreiter writes that the various categories and terms for "popular religion" suggest that "religion is immensely complex and inextricably woven through the fabric of human life. It is not a clear, isolated segment of social life."[56] The final implication here is that the study of popular religion falls within the larger category of religion in general. Thus attempts to interrelate popular religious practices and official liturgy need to consider and be open to the complexity of worship experiences and expressions in everyday life.

Summary

Peter Phan's provocative proposal recasts how we may approach the liturgy as source and summit of Christian life by stretching beyond the boundaries of official liturgy in order to consider its interrelationship with popular religion. He recognizes and maintains the importance and centrality of the eucharistic liturgy as it is experienced in the life of the church, but asks if the *mantra* that the

---

[55] Ibid.
[56] Ibid.

liturgy is the summit and source of church life has led to "one-sided theological interpretations and skewed pastoral practices." Phan argues for a more adequate metaphor, one that better accounts for dynamic interaction between the liturgy, especially the Eucharist, and other activities of the church. He draws on the writings of Karl Rahner as a means to develop a new term, "the liturgy of life," writing that the liturgy of life is the summit and source of the church's liturgy and popular religion. He then turns to the discipline of sacramental theology in order to show that the liturgy of the church is a "real symbol" of the liturgy of life. He concludes that "the liturgy of life and the liturgy of the church constitute the one worship that humanity renders to God and whose center and supreme fulfillment is Jesus Christ."[57]

Everyday mystical encounters with God (which include Christian moral behavior) account for the larger framework of the liturgy of life, since it is "made possible by God's self-gift embracing the whole human history, always and everywhere." Further, the liturgy of life remains *centered in Christ* because "Jesus' sacrifice on the cross or his liturgy derived its origin or emerged from the liturgy of the world" and "the incarnation, death, and resurrection of the Logos brought it [the liturgy of life] to its fullest fulfillment and constitute its supreme point."[58] Thus while Phan concludes that the liturgy of life is the summit and source of the liturgy of the church, he qualifies this by stating that the summit, source, and center of *both* the liturgy of life *and* the liturgy of the church is "Jesus Christ, who in his incarnation, ministry, death, and resurrection brought God's self-communication to the world to it irrevocable, irreversible, and victorious fulfillment."[59] At the same time, he admits, toward the end of his chapter, that "[i]t is impossible to offer within the remaining space anything remotely approaching an adequate theological treatment of popular religion, especially its relationship to the church liturgy."[60]

[57] Phan, "Liturgy of Life," 272.
[58] Ibid., 270.
[59] Ibid., 273.
[60] Ibid., 274.

We turned to the work of Robert Schreiter, who, along with Mark Francis, reveals the inadequacy of the dual terms "popular religion" and "popular piety," often used interchangeably in church documents and theological writings to describe and group together all non-official worship practices. Schreiter's three considerations for the construction of a theological method for popular religion remain helpful to the goals of this book: (1) consideration of the place and voice of non-official, nonelite, and nonexpert people; (2) an examination of the lived worship experiences of these people that move "beyond the text"[61] of liturgical and doctrinal statements; (3) an awareness of the complexity of all worship practices under the broader category of religion.

Thus far we have brought into dialogue interdisciplinary perspectives from the pioneers of the liturgical movement, official documents, and critical reflections by liturgical theologians. We have also heard some of the stories from my ethnographic participants that helped bring to bear the voices and *lived* worship experiences of the laity and got a glimpse of how they came to interpret the interrelationship between official liturgy and the various worship practices in which they engage in everyday life. To help us explore that direction even more deeply, the next chapter will present a primer on the sociology of lived religion, which serves as the primary scientific tool in our investigation.

[61] The reference here is to Lawrence A. Hoffman, who responds to past approaches to liturgical studies that emphasized philological analyses of liturgical texts to the detriment of understanding the actual ritual practices that people *do* during worship events. The "formal object of liturgical studies" is not so much the *texts* of liturgy as it is the "living [breathing] offering praying church." See his *Beyond the Text: A Holistic Approach to Liturgy* (Bloomington: Indiana University Press, 1987), 1, with reference to Robert Taft's "Response to the Berakah Award: Anamnesis," *Worship* 59 (1985): 305–25.

Chapter Five

Mapping Out the Sociocultural Context for Everyday Worship, Religion, and Spirituality

"God is my source," Rachel Durst responds quickly. I had asked her, "who or what is the source of your life?" She explains that, for her, there are "three experiences of God as source": "the God of my personal prayer . . . the God of my church community, and the God of my family." These "three experiences" form the basis of her everyday worship practices, which consist of "chats with God" while driving in the car, Sunday Eucharist at St. Agnes, meal prayers with her family, and prayers with her students [her "extended family"] in the classroom.

Rachel describes her "chats with God" while driving as her personal prayer. These include her trips to St. Agnes or to the high school. Other chats occur while she is "doing chores." "I get into that one since I love to chat a lot." Her image of God is "the God who is always present to me at any moment of my life, any moment where joy, sorrow, excitement happens." I found these "spiritual chats" very intriguing and asked her to explain a bit more.

Rachel: I mean, we all talk to ourselves. There is a difference between just talking to myself and putting myself in the presence of God, making myself *aware* that God is present always.

Ricky: So, if I were to videotape you "chatting with God," what would I actually see?

Rachel: You probably wouldn't see anything different than me going about my chores. It's in my imagination; it's in my heart, because my heart gets engaged as well. You know, if I'm upset about something, it's not just the thoughts but the emotions as well.

Ricky: Do you talk aloud? Do you hear God talking to you?"

Rachel: I think it's very much like mental talking to oneself. However, there are times when I realize that some of the conversation is taking the direction I don't think I would've taken on my own. . . . I think that the direction of my conversation just takes place, takes me to places I wouldn't go otherwise. And it takes me to places where I wouldn't go if I weren't taking that conscious time to put myself in God's presence.

Rachel's second type of experience of God as source is "God in church," namely, Sunday Eucharist, which she divides into "listening to the word" (the first half of Mass) and the Eucharist (the second half of the Mass). For Rachel, these occasions allow her to get "in touch with people [she doesn't] know," since it is "representative of the whole church community." She explains:

Rachel: I need this as part of the person that I am.

Ricky: What is the "this"?

Rachel: My relationship with God and the community, to help me be faithful to my relationship with God. And I need to be reminded what my commitment is and how to live that out, and to be challenged and to be faithful.

Finally, within domestic settings, ritual meal blessings are the best example of a time when Rachel experiences "the God in family." When I visited her and Mark in their home for dinner one evening, Mark led the meal blessing, which consisted of our holding hands around the dinner table and listing our petitions, followed by a short blessing of the meal. "So in that way," Rachel explains, "we bring our concerns, we bring our petitions."

In noting the distinction between all of these types of worship practices, she explains:

Rachel: Classroom prayers are more formulaic, [such as] the prayer of St. Francis. Or sometimes we bring petitions. At dinnertime it's [about] bringing petitions . . . before [we eat] the meal. And Mass is liturgical prayer. And when I'm doing chores, many times it's these chats. And before going to sleep it's more about entrusting all of the worries of the day.

In relating all of her worship experiences of God, she concludes, "It's the same God, but different experiences of that same God."

❖ ❖ ❖

During my second interview with Jude Penland, I asked her again if there was a specific prayer ritual, besides Sunday Eucharist, that connects her to St. Agnes in the same or a different way than her recitation of Vespers connects her to Our Lady of the Rock monastery. You may recall that Jude is an oblate member of this Episcopalian community, which she visits two to three times a year. She describes how she prays the prayer booklet, *The Sacred Space*. These booklets are distributed in the hospitality space of St. Agnes during the seasons of Advent and Lent:

Jude: I love those, I have to admit. I keep mine in my bathroom! [She laughs.] So, especially with my mom dying [March 2012], my mind was such a wreck. There was no way I could do my Office. *The Sacred Space* booklets are, you know: it's like a first-grade primer compared to the Office. And in that time in my life I needed the first-grade primer. And so it was perfect! That's one way I connect to the St. Agnes community ritually.

Ricky: It sounds as if you have two worshiping communities in your life . . .

Jude: I do. I have a foot in each world. My St. Agnes life is *that* world, and the monastery with the Benedictines is *the other* world. In my mind it's all blended. It's like I don't see this hole between separated communities anymore, other than the geographical—one is in California, the other's in Washington. They flow just as easily . . .

Ricky: Is there any "moment" when you realize that this "flowing" is occurring? Are you ever consciously aware of such moments?

Jude: I would say not 24/7 outside of when I'm doing them (saying the Office), or outside of being at Mass, like participating in the eucharistic church. Yes, it all comes and goes. This is my prayerful life. It's also what defines me.

❖   ❖   ❖

I asked Edward Williams what makes Alcoholics Anonymous "spiritual" [his term]. He noted that the meetings open with the recitation of "the serenity prayer" and close with the Our Father. Second, AA meetings are opportunities for transformation:

> I think of it like a movement in effect, that it's in a hundred and some countries, that [it] transforms lives and, in fact, transforms communities. So AA itself is altering the world [and] the person; [it's] changing the life of the person.

He later comments:

> The stated purpose . . . of AA is to help one have a "spiritual awakening." I find it spiritual because it is nourishing and protective and is dependent upon helping others, a common bond. It's a community of committed individuals.

❖   ❖   ❖

In the introduction to this book I traced how, after the Second Vatican Council, liturgical theologians drew mainly on anthropological tools in order to privilege and/or consider the contextual locus for liturgy. By way of examples, I referenced Margaret Mary Kelleher's study of the ritual context of the communion rite as it was performed by a specific worshiping community, and Anscar

Chupungco's development of methods that accounted for the cultural needs of the local church, which were then carefully balanced with the substantial unity of the European cultural tradition as represented by adherence to the typical editions. I also demonstrated the ecumenical scope of liturgical scholars' continued borrowing of anthropological tools in order to consider the local cultural contexts of worship practices. For *liturgical* theologians the starting point and focus has always been *the liturgy*. The "cultural turn" within the field of liturgical studies that emerged out of the Second Vatican Council presumed that the starting point *of liturgy* is to be found *within the ritual event itself*—i.e., as it transpires within official prescriptive and geographical boundaries—to the detriment of considering more seriously how the contextual locus of liturgy may be found elsewhere, that is, *beyond the boundaries* of official institutional praxis.

While I am deeply indebted to these scholars who stretched the methodological boundaries of liturgical studies to include the social sciences, and while I am also informed by the outcome of their research, this book asks new questions: How do the manifold religious/spiritual practices that Christian people cultivate create a continuum with their participation in more official liturgical rites, and what kind of reciprocal interactions and mutual influences are/are not created along this continuum? We have already seen how this continuum can be understood theologically, using the work of Peter Phan on the liturgy of life as source and summit of Christian life. What additional perspectives might sociology and ethnography add, and how do they stretch the contextual horizon of the study of "liturgy"?

To date, only a handful of liturgical studies have used sociological tools. One example is Kieran Flanagan's *Sociology and Liturgy: Re-presentations of the Holy* (1991). However, Flanagan writes not as a theologian but as a sociologist addressing the discipline of liturgical studies.[1] A few studies by liturgists, such as

---

[1] Kieran Flanagan, *Sociology and Liturgy: Re-presentations of the Holy* (New York: St. Martin's Press, 1991). Flanagan admits that his work is not to uncover theological implications, but he asks how the study of public enacted liturgical rites (e.g., the Roman Catholic Mass) may contribute to the field of sociology:

"The Notre Dame Study of Catholic Parish Life,"[2] made use of
sociological tools, but these approaches were based primarily in
either demographic/statistical inquiries or in historical studies,
without attempts to articulate theological implications.[3] Among the
reasons why others have not drawn upon the sociological disciplines was that the field, by and large, did not provide interdisciplinary tools for cultural interpretation, the focus of liturgical
ferment following the Second Vatican Council.[4]

"Although sociology cannot certify the spiritual efficacy of a particular form of
rite, whether it 'works' or not, it does have a prejudice in favour of liturgical
styles that seems to best reflect existing sociological assumptions about how to
understand religious rituals" (p. 7). Also, his lack of knowledge of the liturgical reforms that emerged from the Second Vatican Council, most notably,
SC's call for "full, conscious, and active participation" (art. 14) and cultural
adaptation (arts. 37–40) becomes apparent in his criticisms, as he admits to his
own "obvious bias *against* liberal theological assumptions regarding cultural
elements that impinge on liturgical operations" (p. 8, emphasis in original).
He continues: "These latter tend to stress an informality of style so that formal
ceremonial aspects are minimised to maximise active participation, to pre-
serve a democratic quality in rite that is culturally sensitive, which includes all
and precludes none. Symbols and acts are kept as intelligible as possible and
ambiguity is regarded as being counterproductive. One of the aims of this
analysis is to argue against this liberal consensus regarding liturgical styles of
enactment and to suggest that it is sociologically misconceived" (p. 8).

[2] See Mark Searle, "The Notre Dame Study of Catholic Parish Life," *Worship*
60 (1986): 312–33. Searle writes: "Sociology is not, and probably should not be,
a creative or inventive discipline. It seeks rather to identify, describe and analyze significant aspects of life in the human community, matters about which
most alert participants in social life have more or less accurate impressions
already" (p. 312).

[3] This includes Martin D. Stringer, *A Sociological History of Christian Worship*
(Cambridge: Cambridge University Press, 2005) and Frank C. Senn, *The People's
Work: A Social History of the Liturgy* (Minneapolis: Fortress Press, 2006).

[4] In reference to the 1970s, William H. Sewell reminds us: "Anthropology
. . . had a virtual monopoly on the concepts of culture. In political science and
sociology, culture was associated with the by then utterly sclerotic Parsonian
theoretical synthesis. The embryonic 'cultural studies' movement was still
confined to a single research center in Birmingham. And literary studies were
still fixated on canonical literary tests—although the methods of studying
them were being revolutionized by the importation of 'French' structuralist
and post-structuralist theory. Moreover, the mid-1960s to the mid-1970s were

In the remainder of this chapter I will present a primer on a subfield of sociology, namely, the sociology of lived religion, and reference the works of Robert A. Orsi, David D. Hall, Nancy T. Ammerman, Meredith B. McGuire, Giuseppe Giordan, and William H. Swatos, Jr. The works of these sociologists and others serve as the primary social scientific tools of this book and provide one of the methodological foundations for the next chapter, which focuses on my ethnographic research project.

The Sociology of Lived Religion and the Everyday Practices of Religiosities and Spiritualities

Since its beginnings the discipline of sociology has taken seriously the relationship between religion and societal analysis.[5]

---

the glory years of American cultural anthropology . . . Not only did anthropology have no serious rivals in the study of culture, but the creativity and prestige of cultural anthropology were at a very high point." Sewell, "The Concept(s) of Culture," 152–74 in idem, *Logics of History: Social Theory and Social Transformation* (Chicago: University of Chicago Press, 2005), 153. The concept of culture as a *qualitative* tool for social analysis did not begin to be fully recognized until the mid-1980s. During this period there emerged among sociologists a groundswell of interest in cultural studies. See: Victoria E. Bonnell and Lynn Hunt, eds., *Beyond the Cultural Turn* (Berkeley: University of California Press, 1999). Bonnell and Hunt note other important thinkers and their works during this time period, including Roland Barthes, *Mythologies*, trans. Annette Lavers (New York: Hill and Wang, 1972); Pierre Bourdieu, *Outline of a Theory of Practice*, trans. Richard Nice (Cambridge: Cambridge University Press, 1977), and idem, *Distinction: A Social Critique of the Judgment of Taste*, trans. Richard Nice (Cambridge, MA: Harvard University Press, 1984); Jacques Derrida, *Of Grammatology*, trans. Gayatri Chakravorty Spivak (Baltimore: Johns Hopkins University Press, 1976); Michel Foucault, *The Order of Things: An Archaeology of the Human Sciences* (New York: Vintage Books, 1970), idem, *The Archaeology of Knowledge and the Discourse on Language*, trans. A. M. Sheridan Smith (New York: Pantheon Books, 1972), and idem, *Discipline and Punish: The Birth of the Prison*, trans. Alan Sheridan (New York: Vintage Books, 1977); Marshall Sahlins, *Culture and Practical Reason* (Chicago: University of Chicago Press, 1976); and Raymond Williams, *Marxism and Literature* (Oxford: Oxford University Press, 1977).

[5] Randall Collins names three traditions that have emerged from the classical tradition of the sociology of religion: the reductionist or illusionist tradition,

This includes sociologists who have placed religious studies in more intentional dialogue with everyday life,[6] otherwise known as "lived religion." The American roots of this field of inquiry may be traced back to September 1994 when a group made up mainly of

---

religion as social order and morality, and religion as organization and carrier group. He cross-references the works of Karl Marx (1818–83), Émile Durkheim (1858–1917), and Max Weber (1864–1920), social theorists who are considered the founders of this discipline. See his "The Classical Tradition in Sociology of Religion," 19–38 in *The Sage Handbook of the Sociology of Religion*, eds. James A. Beckford and N. J. Demerath III (London: Sage Publication, 2007). See also Grace Davie, "The Evolution of the Sociology of Religion: Theme and Variation," 61–75 in *The Handbook of the Sociology of Religion*, ed. Michele Dillon (Cambridge: Cambridge University Press, 2003).

[6] What demarcates "the everyday" has been the subject of numerous sociological studies and debates. For example, Norbert Elias (1897–1990) suggested that, in the past, sociological concepts of the "everyday" had been framed in the *negative*: the "everyday" was made up of those aspects of social life that remained outside or around the borders of mainstream sociological focal points. See his "On the Concept of Everyday Life," 166–74 in *The Norbert Elias Reader: A Biographical Selection*, eds. Johan Goudsblom and Stephen Mennell (Oxford: Blackwell, 1998). As Henri Lefebvre (1901–1991) framed it, everyday life may be seen as "the leftovers" of those structured activities that had been singled out by analysis. Among Lefebvre's more important works, see his *Critique of Everyday Life*, trans. John Moore (London: Verso, 1991). Another early example of an "everyday approach" to sociology came from Erving Goffman (1922–1982). In *The Presentation of Self in Everyday Life*, Goffman developed a theory in which social actors, in their performance of everyday life activities—in settings ranging from the domestic to the workplace to the marketplace—were influenced by their physical location or, as he suggests, by the "front and back regions." "Regions" were places that were "bounded to some degree by barriers to perception" and where performances took place. Goffman helped alter our perception of everyday action by considering those aspects of the everyday that we do not ordinarily see but that nonetheless remain influential for our overall perception. See his *The Presentation of Self in Everyday Life* (New York: Anchor Books, 1959). In a more recent assessment Ben Highmore continues this line of thinking by suggesting that a sociology of everyday life shifts the location from where theoretical construction usually occurs toward social activities that are often neglected. See his "Introduction: Questioning Everyday Life," 1–34 in *The Everyday Life Reader*, ed. Ben Highmore (New York: Routledge, 2002).

historians of religion and a few ethnographers was invited to Harvard Divinity School in Cambridge, Massachusetts, for a conference known as "the lived religion project."[7] The project, headed by David D. Hall, who collected and edited the papers from this conference under the title *Lived Religion in America*, focused on how Christians practiced their religious beliefs in everyday life during different time periods of American history: "While we know a great deal about the history of theology and (say) church and state," they agreed, "we know next-to-nothing about religion as practiced and precious little about the everyday thinking and doing of lay men and women."[8]

Since the conference, an academic trajectory of sociologists of religion has explored other avenues of inquiry regarding religion and everyday life, including Nancy Ammerman, Giuseppe Giordan, Stephen Hunt, Gordon Lynch, Meredith McGuire, Jolyon Mitchell, Mary Jo Neitz, Robert Orsi, Anna Strhan, and William Swatos.[9]

---

[7] The lived religion project was part of a larger grant project funded by the Lilly Endowment, *Protestantism and Cultural Change in American History*, which sponsored the works of William R. Hutchinson "on the changing relationship of the Protestant religious establishment to pluralism in America from the colonial period to the present" and Hall's project on lived religion. Participants of the lived religion project included Nancy T. Ammerman, Anne S. Brown, Cheryl Forbes, Rebecca Kneale Gould, R. Marie Griffith, Danièle Hervieu-Léger, Michael McNally, Robert Orsi, Stephen Prothero, and Leigh Eric Schmidt. This project consisted of five interrelated phases: "an initial period of informal consultation; a course in the Harvard Divinity School curriculum on lived religion; support for individual research projects; two major conferences in September 1994 and May 1996," and the publication of revised conference papers in *Lived Religion in America: Toward a History of Practice*, ed. David D. Hall (Princeton, NJ: Princeton University Press, 1997). See http://www.resourcingchristianity.org/grant-project/protestantism-and-cultural-change-in-american-history.

[8] David D. Hall, "Introduction," in *Lived Religion in America*, vii.

[9] A listing of works in this field would include Stephen Hunt, *Religion and Everyday Life* (New York: Routledge, 2005); *Everyday Religion: Observing Modern Religious Lives*, ed. Nancy T. Ammerman (Oxford: Oxford University Press, 2007); Meredith McGuire, *Lived Religion: Faith and Practice in Everyday Life* (Oxford: Oxford University Press, 2008); *Religion, Spirituality and Everyday Practices*, ed. Giuseppe Giordan and William H. Swatos (New York and

During their gatherings, the participants of the "the lived religion project" sought to rethink traditional binary approaches that
pitted "official religion" against "popular religion." Lived religion,
instead, is located midway between these two oppositional categories; that is, it occupies "the space . . . between official or learned
Christianity and profane (or 'pagan') culture."[10] Their intention was
to challenge past approaches to popular religion that presumed a
high-low distinction "in which 'official religion' was authoritative
and 'real,' in contrast to popular religion, which was presented as
constituted by unofficial and even degraded forms."[11] Further, two
perspectives on lived religion were brought to bear within this
middle space: (1) that lay people enjoy "a certain measure of au-
tonomy," and (2) that religion encompasses "a range of possibilities, some with the sanction of official religion and others not, or
perhaps ambiguously so."[12] The idea of a range of possibilities is
drawn from practice theory, which the participants saw as an important tool for the study of lived religion: "As most of us use the
term, it encompasses the tensions, the ongoing struggle of definition, which are constituted within every religious tradition and
that are always present in how people choose to act."[13] Finally,
the participants in the project drew on three other lines of inquiry,
including Ammerman's congregation studies,[14] ritual studies, and
the symbolic anthropology of Geertz.

Heidelberg: Springer, 2011), and particularly Mary Jo Neitz's entry in *Lived
Religion in America*, 45–56, "Lived Religion: Signposts of Where We Have Been
and Where We Can Go from Here."

[10] *Lived Religion in America*, viii.

[11] Neitz, "Signposts," 47. Neitz goes even further and suggests that "popular
religion" is often "tainted by associations with racists and colonial writings."

[12] *Lived Religion in America*, viii.

[13] Ibid., xi. Neitz ("Signposts," 47) also draws on practice theory "as a way
of recognizing both the regulatory effects of habitual ways of doing things
and, at the same time, the possibility of innovation."

[14] Hall makes reference to Ammerman's *Bible Believers: Fundamentalists in the
Modern World* (New Brunswick, NJ: Rutgers University Press, 1987). For other
congregational studies see: *Studying Congregations: A New Handbook*, eds.,
Nancy T. Ammerman, Jackson W. Carroll, Carl S. Dudley, and William
McKinney (Nashville: Abingdon Press, 1998), and Mark Chaves, *Congregations
in America* (Cambridge, MA: Harvard University Press, 2004).

Hall named Robert Orsi's 1985 work, *The Madonna of 115th Street*, as "the single most important example" of "doing history."[15] In that work Orsi studied the annual *festa* of the Madonna of Mount Carmel in East Harlem, New York, as Italian immigrants and subsequent generations from 1880 to 1950 celebrated it. But while Orsi explicated "the multiple, overlapping, even contradictory meanings embodied in a symbolic figure," he also paved the way toward a "religion in the streets" approach that considered more intentionally the idea of religion as *lived* experience. In his 2002 introduction to the second edition of *The Madonna of 115th Street*, Orsi writes:

> The study of lived religion situates all religious creativity within culture and approaches all religion as lived experience, theology no less than lighting a candle for a troubled loved one; spirituality as well as other, less culturally sanctioned forms of religious expression (such as licking the stones of a church floor). Rethinking religion as a form of cultural work, the study of lived religion directs attention to institutions *and* persons, texts *and* rituals, practice *and* theology, things *and* ideas—all as media of making and unmaking worlds. . . . Religious practices and understandings have meaning only in relation to other cultural forms and in relation to the life experiences and actual circumstances of the people using them; what people mean and intend by particular religious idioms can be understood only situationally, on a broad social and biographical field, not within the terms of a religious tradition or religious language understood as existing apart from history.[16]

While the lived religion project took up these questions through historical lenses, the need for an application of this emerging sociological line of inquiry to more modern times was quickly apparent. Nancy Ammerman's edited volume, *Everyday Religion: Observing Modern Religious Lives*, Meredith McGuire's *Lived Religion: Faith and Practice in Everyday Life*, and the more recently edited volume

---

[15] *Lived Religion in America*, ix–x. The reference is to Robert A. Orsi, *The Madonna of 115th Street* (New Haven: Yale University Press, 1985; 2d ed. 2002).

[16] Orsi, "Introduction to the Second Edition," ix–xxxviii in *The Madonna of 115th Street* (2002), at xix–xx.

Religion, Spirituality, and Everyday Practice, by Giuseppe Giordan and William Swatos, remain definitive works in this regard.[17] From the authors of these three volumes I have drawn five principles for enquiry into practices of lived religion:

1. that a new measuring stick be used to study religious and spiritual practices that broadens the definitional boundaries of "religion";

2. that the insights of nonexperts and nonclerical leaders be privileged in the study of lived religion;

3. that researchers assume the interchangeability of the terms and understandings of "religious" and "spiritual";

4. that attention be given to the micro- and macro-level negotiations of the religious and spiritual identities of those studied;

5. that narrative analysis be used as an ethnographic tool in the study of lived religion.

Principles for Enquiry into Practices of Lived Religion

Principle One: We Need a New Measuring Stick for Studying Religious and Spiritual Practices that Broadens the Definitional Boundaries of "Religion"

Given the pervasiveness of worship practices in today's modern life, Ammerman (speaking on behalf of the other contributors to *Everyday Religion*)[18] calls for a new "measuring stick" with which to observe and analyze how people come to practice everyday religion. She notes that older models of measuring the relationship between religion and society[19] led to predictions that blind faith

---

[17] See n. 9 above.

[18] In addition to Nancy Ammerman and Meredith McGuire, the contributors to this volume include Grace Davie, Enzo Pace, Lynn Davidman, Lynn Schofield Clark, Mia Lövheim, Peggy Levitt, Ziad Munson, Paul Lichterman, John P. Bartkowski, Kelly Besecke, and Courtney J. Bender.

[19] Here she quotes Max Weber, who "envisioned a trajectory from Calvinist shopkeepers to heartless capitalists": "The Puritan wanted to work in a calling;

would one day be replaced by reasoned investigation, and religious traditions would soon fade away as secularization increased. As a result, by the mid-twentieth century the measuring stick for religion's impact in society had become a "zero-sum" proposition, postulating that the religious sphere and the secular sphere were "tightly bounded against each other."[20]

The zero-sum proposition may also be seen historically in the relationship between "institutional conceptions of religion" and "personal embodied practices of religion." McGuire reminds us that all "definitional starting points" (i.e., how we come to define what is "religion" or what is "sacred/profane") have always been (and continue to be) social constructions.[21] Referring to the work of Edward Muir, McGuire traces this to the "long Reformation" (roughly 1300–1700 CE), during which time contested social constructions of what defined "religion" among Catholics and Protestants led to "strong negative evaluation of most people's everyday religious practices—especially those that involved their bodies and their emotions." She continues:

> Such embodied practices were important because they were the means by which people had linked the spiritual realm with their pragmatic, quotidian needs—such as healing, fertility, protection from adverse fortune, and obtaining desired material goods.

---

we are forced to do so. For when asceticism was carried out of monastic cells into everyday life, and began to dominate worldly morality, it did its part in building the tremendous cosmos of the modern economic order. . . . But victorious capitalism, since it rests on mechanical foundations, needs its support no longer. . . . In the field of its highest development, in the United States, the pursuit of wealth, stripped of its religious and ethical meaning, tends to become associated with purely mundane passions. . . ." Weber, *The Protestant Ethic and the Spirit of Capitalism* (New York: Scribner, 1958), 181–82, quoted in Ammerman, "Introduction: Observing Modern Religious Lives," 3–19 in *Everyday Religion*, at 3.

[20] Ibid., 9.

[21] McGuire, "Contested Meanings and Definitional Boundaries: Historicizing the Sociology of Religion," 127–38 in *Defining Religion: Investigating the Boundaries between Sacred and Secular*, ed. Arthur L. Greil and David G. Bromley, Religion and the Social Order 10 (Amsterdam: JAI [Elsevier Science], 2003).

After the definitional boundaries around religion were recast, the dominant religious groups in Europe and the Americas came to privilege belief over practice. This definitional bias is now as taken for granted that people commonly refer to religions as "creeds" or "faiths."[22]

For her part, Ammerman sees past approaches to defining religion as limited to "beliefs, memberships, organizational participation [e.g., liturgical participation], and (occasional) experiences and practices." She continues, "These methodologies . . . privilege religious adherence and institutional affiliation as measures of religion's strength."[23]

These sociologists suggest that the boundaries between the sacred and the secular, between institutional definitional boundaries of what constitute religious practices and what constitute individual embodied expressions of religious beliefs, are quite permeable. This is due in part to the plurality of religious and spiritual practices, including those that may be considered "impure" by religious institutions. Such practices do not necessarily lead to the demise of religion's presence and significance in society. Thus, contrary to past "zero-sum" propositions, the manifestations of religious practices and behaviors today cannot be narrowed down to the results of quantitative surveys that list how many people "attend" worship services that are often presumed to be institutionally bounded.

The permeability and fluidity of religious boundaries lead to overlapping and intersecting religious practices that consequently extend definitional boundaries of what constitutes "religion." These sociologists do not subscribe to earlier theories that compartmentalize social domains, presuming, in turn, that there is no inter-

[22] Meredith McGuire, "Embodied Practices: Negotiation and Resistance," 187–200 in *Everyday Religion*, at 189, referencing Edward Muir, *Ritual in Early Modern Europe* (Cambridge and New York: Cambridge University Press, 1997; 2d ed. 2005).

[23] Nancy T. Ammerman, "Studying Everyday Religion: Challenges for the Future," 219–38 in *Everyday Religion*, at 223.

action between domains. "Each domain colors the other," since a variety of domains "often exhibit spiritual influences . . . [and] have failed to become spiritually neutral."[24] Thus worship practices, which include devotional, spiritual, and/or institutionally prescribed rituals, "may happen in unpredictable places."[25]

Principle Two: The Privileging of Nonexperts and Nonclerical Leaders in the Study of Lived Religion

As I noted earlier, in order to move beyond past approaches to popular religion that presumed a high-low distinction that differentiated between "official religion" and "popular religion," sociologists of lived religion more often than not focus on the everyday worship practices of "nonexperts," that is, "the people who do not make a living being religious or thinking and writing about religious ideas . . . among both privileged and nonprivileged people." A sampling of ethnographic participants found in McGuire's *Lived Religion: Faith and Practice in Everyday Life* reveals a mélange of backgrounds, including a married man with four children who lives in a "near-slum neighborhood on the east coast," "belongs" to a Unitarian Church, participates in the services of an Episcopal church, and considers "his extensive social activism to be the most important part of his spirituality"; a baptized Lutheran woman, raised in Ohio, who has been "highly engaged in religious practices and experiences not connected with any official religious group," and whose daily worship service is gardening; a self-proclaimed "nondenominational" man whose worship life centers around twelve-step spirituality; a middle-aged Catholic Latina from Texas who nurtures her spirituality by meditating an hour each morning ("as soon as her children left for school") and through the use of her *"altarcito"* ("home altar") that displays several traditional items, including a family heirloom cross, pictures of deceased or distant loved ones, eighteen candles, wildflowers, an amulet (*milagro*), as well as nontraditional items such as amethyst crystals for healing meditations, Asian incense, a Tibetan prayer

---

[24] Ammerman, "Introduction," *Everyday Religion*, 9.
[25] Ibid.

bell, a Frida Kahlo triptych, and a modern representation of the Virgin of Guadalupe.[26]

As Ammerman reminds us, focus on nonexperts does not discount the value of considering the role of religious institutions, nor does it suggest that "official" ideas are never important. Rather, official ideas

> are most interesting to us once they get used by someone other than a professional. Similarly, everyday implies the activity that happens outside organized religious events and institutions, but that does not mean that we discount the influence those institutions wield or that we neglect what happens within organized religion "every day."[27]

I would add "nonclerical leaders" to the term "nonexperts" since some of the studies in the volumes referenced here consider "theological experts" who may not be in positions of clerical leadership as it applies within the Roman Catholic Church. In "Workers in the Vineyard: Catholic Women and Social Action,"[28] Cathy Holtmann presents her study of almost one hundred Roman Catholic women from New Brunswick, Canada, based on her exploration of how these women came to incorporate their experiences of lived religion into social action. Among her participants were sixteen female members of religious communities "with advanced theological education."[29] Holtmann learned that while these women engaged in practices of social action, contradictions arose over issues of reconciling their "engaged spirituality" with the teaching authority of the church. In time they began "to apply the knowledge and skills they had acquired in social movements to the problem of their religious agency as women in the Catholic Church."[30] Eventually they

---

[26] McGuire, *Lived Religion: Faith and Practice*, 6–10.

[27] Ammerman, "Introduction," *Everyday Religion*, 5.

[28] Cathy Holtmann, "Workers in the Vineyard: Catholic Women and Social Action," 141–52 in Giordan and Swatos, eds., *Religion, Spirituality, and Everyday Practice*.

[29] Ibid., 146.

[30] Ibid.

developed and maintained supportive links of solidarity among themselves.[31] One of Holtmann's concluding points succinctly expresses how overlapping practices of official and non-official leaders may sometimes lead to tensions between individual spirituality and institutional religion:

> An engaged spirituality for Catholic women that includes personal spiritual growth, institutional participation and social action necessarily means a spirituality that is critical of the unjust structures of the contemporary Catholic church. Putting Catholic social teachings into practice becomes problematic for women and for the institutional church because doing so exposes a fundamental contradiction between the church's social teachings and its practice.[32]

The numerous subjects found throughout these three volumes demonstrate that nonexperts and non-official institutional leaders regularly engage in their own forms of religious practices that may not be noticed otherwise or, as in the case of the women in Holtmann's study, challenge institutional authority and/or established practices.

Principle Three: The Interchangeability of the Terms and Understandings of "Religious" and "Spiritual"
One of the themes that often comes up in these works is whether the terms "religious" and "spiritual" are interchangeable or, as Swatos and Giordan describe it, the perceived "religious-spiritual contrast."[33] While acknowledging the complex history of how

[31] She writes (p. 146): "The women in this study chose to join a movement for Catholic religious reform in order to support one another collectively and to receive support from other Catholics in exercising all forms of their religious agency. They used their experiences of religious agency in the realm of social action to critique and work for change in terms of women's opportunities for religious agency within the institution."

[32] Ibid., 151.

[33] In the introduction to their book Swatos and Giordan write: "These chapters take up the religious-spiritual contrast specifically through investigations into *practice*: In what ways do people who claim to be 'religious' or 'spiritual'

Western Christian writers and thinkers came to define "spirituality" (often in contrast to "religion"),[34] most of these sociologists promote an approach that is more in line with Wade Clark Roof's call for an integrated analysis of both terms. Roof borrows Robert Wuthnow's observation that practices of religion, over the past half-century, have led to juxtapositions of "dwelling" and "seeking," particularly in practices of lived religion. Roof suggests that "dwelling" and "seeking" are better viewed as "modes of apprehending the spiritual, either through existing ritual and symbolic systems or through more open-ended, exploratory ways."[35]

Sociologists of lived religion suggest a method that pays closer attention to how ethnographic participants sometimes use these terms interchangeably. For example, one of Ammerman's investigative questions in her own research includes: "When and where do we find experiences that participants define as religious or spiritual?" McGuire admittedly uses the terms "religiosity" and

---

define these self-images as manifest in their own lives? How do people who make this contrast believe people who see themselves in these ways implement their convictions in practice (or should implement them)? We also explore whether there are institutions of spiritual practice to which those who term themselves 'spiritual' turn or whether the difference implied by these terms may instead be between institutionalized and de-institutionalized expressions of practice, including but not limited to self-spiritualities." See "Introduction: The Spiritual 'Turn' in Religion as Process and Outcome," xi–xv in *Religion, Spirituality and Everyday Practice*, at xi.

[34] Linda Woodhead names five historical aspects: (1) early spirituality as a radicalization and "Easternization" of liberal Christianity, (2) ritual, esotericism and nativism in Christianity and spirituality, (3) New Age and its parallels with charismatic-evangelical Christianity, (4) the holistic turn in spirituality and its links to "lived" religion in the West, and (5) contemporary neo-Paganism and its links with Christian tradition, ritual, and place. See her "Spirituality and Christianity: The Unfolding of a Tangled Relationship," 3–21 in *Religion, Spirituality and Everyday Practice*.

[35] Robert Wuthnow, *After Heaven: Spirituality in America Since the 1950s* (Princeton, NJ: Princeton University Press, 1998), 3, quoted in Wade Clark Roof, "Religion and Spirituality: Toward an Integrated Analysis," 137–50 in *A Handbook of the Sociology of Religion*, ed. Michele Dillon (Cambridge and New York: Cambridge University Press, 2003), at 138–39.

"spirituality" interchangeably "to refer to how individuals attend to matters of the religious or the spiritual, as *they* understand those matters at a particular time and context, in their own lives" (emphasis added). She continues:

> We need always to be alert to the social meanings behind such distinctions, because making distinctions involves trying to delineate acceptable from unacceptable beliefs and practices, desirable from denigrated identities and statuses, and worthy from unworthy ideals and values. Religious organizations routinely try to shape such boundaries, exerting their authority to distinguish what they approve as proper individual religious practice from all else.[36]

Closely connected to this is the borrowing and interchanging of cultural resources between institutional religions and people's individual spiritual practices; people who engage in practices of lived religion often choose and deploy material resources (sacred images, prayers, rituals, and so on) that may or may not stem from religious institutions, and/or choose and deploy more "idea-centered" resources, such as religious discourses, memories, and histories. The people we have met in the field are more and less attentive to spiritual matters, but what they see and hear and do when they do pay attention is often subtly shaped by the institutions that have carried dominant religious traditions in those places. Even intensely "personal" mystical experiences "are likely to contain significant strands of image and symbol borrowed from the recognized theologies of the day."[37]

Ammerman and the other authors in *Everyday Religion* prefer to use "religiosities" as an umbrella term that takes into account the plurality of religious and spiritual practices. I prefer to add the term "spiritualities" alongside Ammerman's use of the term "religiosities" in order to remain open to how social actors choose to label their own everyday worship practices: e.g., "everyday practices of religiosities and spiritualities." I combine both terms based

---

[36] *Lived Religion*, 6.
[37] Ammerman, "Studying Everyday Religion," in *Everyday Religion*, 219.

on my ethnographic research project wherein my participants often used both terms interchangeably, as Ammerman and McGuire suggest. But even the singular term "religiosities" may presume some level of adherence to institutional location when, for at least one of my participants, no attachment to any Christian institutional structure remained present in his own Daoist sensibility. Daoism as a "religion" continues to be a contested generalized term.[38]

Principle Four: The Micro-Level and Macro-Level Negotiations of Religious and Spiritual Identities

Holtmann's study of Catholic women is a prime example of why sociologists of lived religion use the term "negotiation" as a chief metaphor when examining how their ethnographic participants interchange religious identities and "spiritual options." The "multiple solidarities" that lead to the "permeability of institutional boundaries" may lead to various negotiations of social action that occur "between predictability and improvisation."

We inevitably categorize what we see (if this is an X, then I do Y) and form habitual responses to typical situations. What we do is not simply automatic; it is shaped into "settled dispositions." As we have seen, existing religious schemas have a profound ability to produce predictable "strategies of action." But we have also seen that human actors can invoke those strategies in unpredictable ways and unlikely places. No single situation is ever completely predictable, in part because we constantly import rules and symbols from one situation into another new or unfamiliar one.[39]

[38] Kwok Pui-lan, "Empire and the Study of Religion" (Presidential Address, American Academy of Religion, Annual Meeting, San Francisco, CA, November 19, 2011).

[39] Ammerman, "Studying Everyday Religion," in *Everyday Religion*, 228, with references to Ann Swidler ["strategies of action"], as employed in her "Culture in Action: Symbols and Strategies," *American Sociological Review* 51 (1986): 273–86, and Courtney Bender ["the importation of rules and symbols"], as in her *Heaven's Kitchen: Living Religion as God's Love We Deliver* (Chicago: University of Chicago Press, 2003).

Two realities need to be taken into account: one remains at the micro-level of negotiation while the other is at the macro-level of public contexts. At the micro-level of negotiation,

> something becomes religious because it is understood to be so by those who observe and participate in it. . . . Whenever people talk about and orient their lives in ways that go beyond everyday modern rationality, when they enchant their lives by drawing on spiritual language and concepts and experiences, they are engaging in religious action.[40]

This ties into McGuire's concern for how we may come to conceptualize individual religious practices. There is a general assumption that individuals commit "to an entire, single package of beliefs and practices of an official religion,"[41] when, in fact, many people come to negotiate a variety of religious and spiritual practices that extend beyond concepts of individual commitment. As a result, "our conceptual apparatus has simply failed to question the image of religious membership and individual religious practice built on mutually exclusive, indeed antagonistic, categories."[42]

At the macro-level and public context, "[d]efinitions of religion exist in cultural, political, historical, and legal contexts that frame what happens in everyday negotiation."[43] A good example of this is seen in Enzo Pace's essay in *Everyday Religion*, "Religion as Communication: The Changing Shape of Catholicism in Europe."[44] Pace contends that even though the Roman Catholic Church has lost all "moral authority, political power, and active participation" in Europe, church leaders continue to harness their religious power through communications media: "They can no longer impose norms, but they can reconstruct a romantic sense of being a society, a collective identity rooted in the Christian pattern of values,

---

[40] Ammerman, "Studying Everyday Religion," in *Everyday Religion*, 224–25.
[41] McGuire, *Lived Religion*, 11.
[42] Ibid., 12.
[43] Ammerman, "Studying Everyday Religion," in *Everyday Religion*, 225.
[44] Enzo Pace, "Religion as Communication: The Changing Shape of Catholicism in Europe," 37–49 in *Everyday Religion*.

projecting unity where there is social, religious, and ideological difference."[45]

Roman Catholicism continues to be a "meaningful world" as 87 percent of Italians and 84 percent of Spaniards continue to call themselves "Catholic."[46] Yet despite these affiliations, most Catholics in these countries increasingly disconnect from the church's moral authority.[47] Their departures from the church's moral teaching, in turn, have led to declines in attendance in official worship services. Pace suggests that observations of their lived religious experiences should rely on their practices of popular religion: "The religiosity of Italians and Spaniards is often found, if at all, outside the walls of the Church. If one can speak of religious recomposition in Spain, it should be sought in the revival of local cults and popular devotions, which enable whole communities to reassert their local identity."[48]

In her attempt to avoid rigid dichotomies between these two levels of negotiations (i.e., the "fuzziness around the edges of categories"), Ammerman suggests some common links between the micro- and macro-levels of religious activities:

> It seems to me that religious activity is recognized as such because it has something to do with things that are sacred, transcendent, or beyond the ordinary. Indeed, in much of what most people take to be religious, there are assumed to be "Sacred Others" (God or gods) at work, and the identity and history of those gods is collectively recognized and legitimated. Action that is understood as religious action is typically embedded in a story about sacred realities and how human beings interact with those realities.[49]

[45] Ibid., 37.

[46] Statistical reference to Rafael Diaz-Salazar, *El capital simbolico: Estructura social, politica y religión en España* (Madrid: HOAC, 1988); Salvador Giner and Salvador Sarasa, eds., *Religión y sociedad en España* (Madrid: CIS, 1993); Patrick Michel, *Politique et Religion: La Grande Mutation* (Paris: Albin Michel, 1996).

[47] Pace, "Religion as Communication," 38.

[48] Ibid., 39, with reference to Marlène Albert-Llorca, "Renouveau de la religion locale," 235–52 in *Identités religieuses en Europe*, eds. Grace Davie and Danièle Hervieu-Léger (Paris: La Découverte, 1996).

[49] Ammerman, "Studying Everyday Religion," in *Everyday Religion*, 225.

Principle Five: Narrative Analysis as an Ethnographic Tool for Study of Lived Religion

Narrative analysis is a popular tool used by these sociologists to conduct ethnographic research. Ammerman writes that, unlike "didactic lessons or moral recipes," which often mark the literature of theological experts and official leaders, narratives allow for the unfolding of plots, characters, relationships, and motivations that often mark the everyday lives of people. These stories may include "ritual interruptions" or other activities that "may be more or less explicit."[50] In a previous study of the links between religious identity and the religious institutional affiliation Ammerman proposed that the study of "narrative construction" allows social scientists to "move past the words themselves" and calls for a closer attention "to the *relationships* and *actions* that give words their meaning."[51]

In his essay in *Everyday Religion*, "Connections and Contradictions: Exploring the Complex Linkages between Faith and Family," John P. Bartkowski examines the marriages and family lives of twenty evangelical Christian males as they attempt to balance "the demands of secular concerns and sacred convictions" that are to be found between "deeply held religious ideals" and "secular culture" and between "everyday household practices" and the "religious convictions that couples hold dear."[52] His primary method of narrative analysis leads to an awareness of how his participants come to describe boundary actions:

---

[50] Ibid., 226.

[51] Emphasis in original. Ammerman writes: "If we are to understand the nature of identity in a complex world that involves multiple solidarities that both constrain and are continually reconstructed, we need a dynamic mode of analysis that moves beyond categorizing words and analyzing syntax . . . Narrative . . . renders an event understandable by connecting it to a set of relationships and practices—historically and spatially, particular people doing socially patterned things." See Nancy T. Ammerman, "Religious Identities and Religious Institutions," 207–24 in *A Handbook of the Sociology of Religion*, at 213.

[52] John P. Bartkowski, "Connections and Contradictions: Exploring the Complex Linkages between Faith and Family," 153–66 in *Everyday Religion*, at 153.

I begin with the premise that narratives are "storied" in two senses. First, narratives are vital for organizing everyday experiences and imbuing life with meaning. Narratives enable storytellers to convey important cultural cues about who they are and who they are not, and to explain why certain courses of action are taken while others are averted. . . . Other narratives draw on the logic of distinction and thereby underscore boundaries between different types of people and experiences. Thus, some narratives employ bridging discourse, while others reflect boundary work.[53]

The second feature of his narrative approach allows for the unveiling of layers of meanings ("storied quality") that often compete with and/or complement one another: "Thus, while narratives are an attempt to impose meaning and order on complicated experiences, they are ineluctably marked by contradictions, tensions, and ironies."

Summary

While my list of five summary points is not exhaustive, it suggests other possibilities for framing the wider sociocultural context within which practices of religiosities and spiritualties occur.
A church building is just one among many such locations. One should also consider domestic, leisure, and workplace locations, particularly since these "social domains" often intersect with one another. Sociologists of lived religion privilege locations outside of institutional boundaries as starting points of inquiry, but they also remain open to how individuals and collective social groups perform these practices within and around these boundaries.
Each social actor and/or social group, in turn, negotiates varying levels of membership, ritual participation, and accountability, often simultaneously.

[53] Ibid., 155.

Chapter Six

A Spectrum of Worship Practices: Ethnographic Method, Interpretations, and Correlations

Irene and James informed me that they do not "go to Mass" often. We were sitting in the living room of their apartment, just two blocks away from St. Agnes, so I asked them how often they *did* go. "On average," James explained, "once every three months." Even this is difficult to specify, they admitted. Sometimes the two young adults go three weeks in a row, then not at all for the next few months. James continues:

> So like going to church: Is it morally right for me to *not* go on Sunday? No. But even though I'm bettering myself to go to church, I think by not going, for the most part, I'm not discrediting my beliefs, or discrediting how much I embrace my God or my religion.

He explains this further by describing a "yin-yang" (his term) approach to Mass:

> Part of what Mass is for me is: I fulfill my spiritual side. My spiritual side is as good as my physical side. And then I get a peace of mind, like, I'm good, like no matter what, from this point to whatever, I'm good because there's no anxiety; there's happiness. I received the Eucharist, or I heard something and it was great. But if I didn't go and I did something constructive, it's the same to me because I still did something positive. And even though I didn't go to church and receive the body of God and the blood of Christ (or anything

like that), I still didn't lose anything of my retention of what religion
is or what God is or what my moral standards are.

Irene agrees with James that their spiritual lives are "not exclusive to [going to Mass] every week." Irene explains that her spiritual life does not consist of a list of prayers, devotions, or formulas, like her "mother's spiritual life." Instead, she describes *moments* when she recognizes God's presence. She calls these moments "this is church!"

Irene: So if I experience something really awesome or radical
            in a moment, I say "this is church!" It could be a crazy
            party or a musical event or we could be, like, in Dolores
            Park. You know what I mean?

I invited her to explain a bit more.

Irene: Maybe it's contemporary. Like we will be with folks at a
            concert or something and we become so submersed in
            the music.

Ricky: What are you feeling during those moments?

Irene: Well, the last time I felt like this, it was the one with DJ
            Crush from Japan. We were at the mezzanine and, like,
            the music was so awesome! You know what I mean?
            The music was *speaking to me*, it was lifting me up . . .

Ricky: So why do you use the term "church"?

Irene: Because God is there; God is there at the moment: move-
            ment, beauty, transformation . . . and because God is
            there, this is church!

James: I've heard her say this before. Like we're eating this
            crazy dinner and we have friends over and she says,
            "This is church!" A "psycho-saying," like, when we are
            doing anything religious. I think it's acknowledging,
            "I love this!"

Irene: I know it's like "Where two or three are gathered in my
            name." It's kinda like that, like a critical mass type of

126

	feeling, but sometimes as intimate as a dinner. Like the time James and I went fishing in Ohio . . . that's church!
Ricky:	Would you say, then, that having these "This is church!" moments are like going to Mass?
Irene:	Actually, yeah, it's like that! It's like the church building is where everything I associate is valuable.

She makes a distinction between "Mass" and "church."

	Sometimes it's two different things. I'll go to *church* more times than I go to *Mass*.
Ricky:	Which means . . .?
Irene:	When I go to church, I could go to St. Ignatius and light a candle. And I think that sometimes with Masses, the same thing; it's a spiritual place. You know God is there. But it's also an invitation to be still, to let God, to feel God. But it could happen at a dinner, you know what I mean? Food is an expression of this too sometimes. What I feel: this is an expression of God, anything great, like a lot of cultural forms. And that's why God is such a cultural person because those are expressions: that awesome innovation is God! So it's the visceral!
Ricky:	So when you say "this is church!" what, then, is your definition of "church"?
Irene:	It's a place that you know God is there. While God can be everywhere, sometimes I'm not present. So it's kind of like that calibration: I'm here; God's here. God is everywhere but sometimes you need to be present to actually feel it. But I think factually, God is everywhere. You could find God anywhere.

Irene also described how sometimes she "takes a photo" on her iPhone during these "this is church!" moments.[1] The photos reveal a variety of settings and contexts: the moment she came across a graffiti scribble on a sign with the words "Let go," which she

[1] See appendix 5, p. 185.

entitled "Homily"; the moment on March 22 when she was visiting Chicago and noticed the vast sky, which she entitled, "Alleluia Sky"; the moment on March 25 when she was planting a pot of jalapeños in her home; the moment on January 26 when she took a picture of the ultrasound image of her baby and discovered, along with James, that she was pregnant.

❖   ❖   ❖

While his wife, Rachel, answered that God is the source and summit of her life, Mark's short answer to my question was "family." In his description of his answer he imagines the setting of his home, where all of his children are present:

> We talk about living sort of a Christian life and that's the place [their home] where we both get the most opportunity to truly do kind things and also where we are most tested. . . . [It's also the place] with the most challenges because we have to deal with people when they're good and when we are not so good.

I ask him why his family within a house setting is "the source." He responds, "I took it in the sense of meaning *what brings you back* . . . something that is a source of nourishment that you just don't have in any other way." I further inquire what this may "look like," and he notes an array of practices through which he communicates with his family: "When I talk with one of the kids on the phone, and I get off the phone and [say to myself] 'That was really good!'" He further explains that he travels a lot, and notes his daily practice of calling Rachel every night. "It's not intellectual nourishment; it's just the feeling of experiencing, you know, loving someone and being loved in return." He does not consider these communication practices "worship practices" *per se*, but says he becomes "*aware*" of their spiritual meaning afterward, when he "process[es] it sometime later." He later suggests that a more ritualized form of "feeling connected" with his family occurs during meal prayers and refers to Rachel's previous description.

Mark's practice of connecting with his family in order to be nourished are directly related to the answer he provides when I ask him what is "the summit of his life." "I thought of different answers with different time frames. So, sorry, but I'm not gonna give you *one answer*. And a lot of it is related to family. Like on the annual cycle, we look forward to the holidays because we are with our families together."

I ask him how he interconnects his practices that connect him with his family and Sunday eucharistic liturgies at St. Agnes. He breaks this down into annual gatherings and weekly gatherings, noting that the yearly gatherings with his family are "knitted to the liturgical season and the [liturgical] services" [that occur during those seasons]:

> We attend most of the big services around the holidays with every-body and they are all there. So it's a sense of being able to share our religious life in a way that we don't usually. . . . Not only do our kids get to participate, but that community [St. Agnes] gets to see them, and around those holidays we sometimes have a dinner, go to a restaurant with some old family friends or something . . . and there's usually a church connection there.

His connection between family and holiday liturgies is so intimate that celebrating Christmas without his family is not the same:

> Christmas presents don't have anything to do with liturgy, but they do have to do with family stressing that they know each other and love each other . . . in the annual sense, it's that if somebody says it's going to be Christmas and there'll be nice people around you, but your entire family is going to be forced to be somewhere else, how is that Christmas? But if someone were to ask "what's the one thing that I have to do in order to have a family gathering?" I would say there has to be a church service somewhere there.

❖   ❖   ❖

In the previous chapters I demonstrated that there are theo-logical, liturgical, and sociological bases for expanding our under-standing of what constitutes "the church's worship" to include not only official rites but also the religious/spiritual practices that are cultivated by engaged Christians. Peter Phan's theological frame-work for understanding liturgy as the "source and summit" of the

Christian life provides a foundation for arguing this theologically. Robert Schreiter's critique of how we define popular religion and popular piety leads to an expansion of our view of worship practices that takes seriously the experiences and voices of non-official, non-elite, and non-expert persons. The forms these worship practices take have come to light throughout the book. Then, drawing on the work of sociologists of religion, we see how their research provides a tool to focus our attention on the many practices and rituals of religiosities and spiritualities (lived religion) in everyday life. Their scholarly perspectives have stretched the cultural mapping of liturgical practice by scholars Mary Collins, Margaret Mary Kelleher, and Anscar Chupungco, whose organic methodological approaches privileged official rites above all other worship practices.

Yet the question remains: how do these theoretical and scholarly perspectives relate to the actual practices and understandings of specific Catholic Christians? If we understand that everyday practices of religiosities and spiritualities are not limited to Sunday Eucharist, we must also take seriously the dynamic interplay that exists among *all* forms of worship, official and non-official, and become aware of their connectedness to and disconnections from one another (how are they related?), the distinctions between them (what makes Sunday Eucharist distinct from all other worship practices?), and the generative influences that emerge from such interactions.

In chapter 1, I introduced the community of St. Agnes Church, providing some background on how many of the parishioners and staff members have come to experience and interpret their Sunday 10:30 AM eucharistic celebrations. Further, at the beginning of each chapter I presented some of the narrative threads that emerged from my ethnographic interviews. These threads will come together in this chapter as I will present the influences and formation of my ethnographic methodology, offer summaries of my interpretations of the interviews, and provide a correlation of these interpretations, followed by a section that demonstrates what we can learn from the participants regarding the interrelationships between everyday worship practices and Sunday eucharistic liturgy.

Influences and Formation of Ethnographic Methodology

My ethnographic methodology accounted for two sets of worship practices (Sunday Eucharist and everyday practices of religiosities and spiritualities) and the interactions that occurred between and among them. I primarily drew upon the work of scholars who, each in his or her own way, consider the porous and fluid boundaries of ethnographic field sites: James Clifford, Mary McGann, and some of the sociologists of religion I referenced in chapter 5.

James Clifford: The Expansion of Ethnographic Field Sites and Terms

As I was formulating an ethnographic methodology for my project I drew on James Clifford's *Routes: Travel and Translation in the Late Twentieth Century*[2] in order to expand my preconceptions of what constitutes an ethnographic field site. The fluidity of observable boundaries needed to be accounted for, and Clifford's "collages" and creative use of images stirred my own investigative imagination. For example, in the prologue to his book, *"In Medias Res,"* Clifford quotes the work of another ethnographer, Amitav Ghosh, who describes his experience of visiting an Egyptian village:

> When I first came to that quiet corner of the Nile Delta I had expected to find on that most ancient and most settled of soils a settled and restful people. I couldn't have been more wrong. The men of the village had all the busy restlessness of airline passengers in a transit lounge. Many of them had worked and travelled in the [sheikdoms] of the Persian Gulf, others had been in Libya and Jordan and Syria, some had been to the Yemen as soldiers, others to Saudi Arabia as pilgrims, a few had visited Europe: some of them had passports so thick they opened out like ink-blackened concertinas.[3]

[2] James Clifford, *Routes: Travel and Translation in the Late Twentieth Century* (Cambridge, MA: Harvard University Press, 1997).

[3] Amitav Ghosh, "The Imam and the Indian," *Granta* 20 (Winter 1986): 135–46, as quoted in Clifford, *Routes*, 1.

This image inspired my own participant observations of Sunday eucharistic liturgies as they were practiced within the physical boundaries of St. Agnes Church. I became attentive to the boundary crossings and transactional dynamics that occurred not only at the entrances and portals of church buildings but also within the worship space itself between "designated sections": for example, the front sanctuary where the immediate actions around the altar occur was placed in conversation with the center transept where the rest of the community assembled; the confessional doors separated "the outside world" from the "inner sanctum" where "private" reconciliation occurred. I also became attentive to how my participants described their own interpretations of boundary crossings between Sunday Eucharist and their everyday worship practices.

I observed that any location for ethnographic inquiry is marked by dwelling and traveling—people coming, people going, and the interplay between cultural "roots" as sociocultural identity and cultural "routes" that flow to and from such locations. Clifford does not dismiss dwelling sites as legitimate centers for scholarly inquiry but instead calls for a more comparative approach between dwelling and traveling that could lead to "new localizations" in which awareness of and attention to borderlines create places for emerging hybridity.

I also needed to learn how Clifford used and even created specific terms so that I might build up a vocabulary for articulating my own ethnographic goals. Ethnography, he contends, challenges the "localism" of common assumptions about space and time. It challenges the concept of culture and, by extension, the rituals that are performed by cultural groups as "circumscribed places" by considering the complexities and the "pervasive spectrum of human experiences." Clifford uses terms such as "translocal" and "transnational" to impress upon the ethnographer's mind the creative images of localization. It is at the "borderlines" of these ever-changing locations that ethnography reveals the dynamic processes of a culture's identity.

In the third part of his book Clifford contends that ethnographic terms such as "border," "travel," "creolization," "transculturation," "hybridity," and "diaspora" are often placed in conversation with "old localizing strategies" that suggest "bounded community," "organic culture," "region," and "center and periphery."[4] He demonstrates how "diasporic forms of longing, memory, and (dis)identification" remain connected yet disconnected from transnational identity formation and suggests that "this overlap of border and diaspora experiences in late twentieth-century everyday life" points to "the difficulty of maintaining exclusivist paradigms."[5] It is terms such as these that helped build my own vocabulary: localism, new localization, roots/routes, circumscribed places, translocal, transnational, and borderlines. More important, these examples became reference points through which I became more attentive to the terms my participants used whenever they needed to describe similar dynamics and experiences.

Mary E. McGann:
Liturgical Ethnography and the Intermezzi *of Time and Space*

Since one set of worship practices that formed the focus of my research involved participant observation of Sunday eucharistic liturgy, I turned to the work of Mary McGann, who has been in the forefront of writing about and conducting research on liturgical ethnography. Her book, *A Precious Fountain: Music in the Worship of an African American Catholic Community,*[6] focuses on the music-making rituals at Our Lady of Lourdes Church in San Francisco, California. Her statement on the purpose of liturgical ethnography greatly informed my own approach to participating in, observing, and transcribing Sunday eucharistic liturgies:

> The purpose of liturgical ethnography is to open to new insight, to receive new paradigms, to make new connections, to welcome fresh deposits of spirit. Its goal is appreciation rather than critique, understanding rather than evaluation. Within the work of liturgical

---

[4] *Routes*, 245.

[5] Ibid., 247.

[6] Mary E. McGann, *A Precious Fountain: Music in the Worship of an African American Catholic Community* (Collegeville, MN: Liturgical Press, 2004).

studies, which necessarily seeks to establish normativity, contemplative ethnographic scholarship can bring to light and reflect on the salience of these new paradigms. For this reason it is integral to the work of critical liturgiology, inviting new paradigms to both confirm and critique our existing normative claims. It introduces new hermeneutics into the fabric of interpretive liturgiology, a process essential to a liturgical scholarship that can truly serve a world church.[7]

I noted her attentiveness to details during ritual moments and ethnographic interviews and her craft of transcribing and conveying these details to her readers. This process informed my own ethnographic method during my participant observation of Sunday eucharistic liturgies, of the everyday worship practices of the participants in my project, and during my interviews with them: for example, careful observation of the delineation of liturgical roles, precise notation of the distance between two points of ritual action, my observations and attentiveness to the words, moods, and feelings that were conveyed by my participants, and the awareness of various ritual sensibilities that worship participants expressed at different moments during official liturgies and everyday worship practices.

McGann does not limit her investigations to the liturgies that transpire *within the walls* of church buildings or the temporal confines of Sunday morning, but also examines how these liturgies remain linked and connected to the wider historical, cultural, and social frameworks of the larger neighborhood and the African American community. This is demonstrated by the layout of her book. While the chapters present a more descriptive and narrative approach to the community's liturgical practices, she inserts five *intermezzi* that expound on more reflective and analytical topics including time, space, words, flow, and embodiment. Specifically, her reflections on "time" (*kairos*) and space as "cosmic geography" provided me with a hermeneutical lens with which to consider

---

[7] Ibid., xx.

how worshipers use liturgical symbols that stretch beyond the temporal and geographical boundaries of official liturgy.[8]

As a liturgical theologian I find myself closely resonating with McGann's scholarly pursuits within the field of liturgical studies. She devotes her final section in *A Precious Fountain* (as well as in another work, *Exploring Music*) to the naming of specific "theological and liturgical understandings and intuitions" that had emerged during her correlation of ethnographic data with Christian sacramental, systematic, and biblical traditions: sacramental worldview, biblical pneumatology, Gospel Christology, ecclesiology of the Body of Christ, and historical/social-political eschatology. Throughout *Precious Fountain* she displays a gift for interweaving a cross-section of theological, narrative, and ritual threads, demonstrating that the awareness of these threads has the potential to influence any theological interpretation of Christian liturgy.

Sociologists of Lived Religion: Ethnographic Approaches to Interrogating the Lived Religious Experiences of Non-Experts

When considering the many practices of religiosities and spiritualities that occur in everyday life, I drew on the ethnographic approaches of the sociologists whose works I examined in chapter 4. Sociologists of lived religion locate themselves within a variety of settings and social contexts, sometimes using and combining a number of resources, including ethnographic data that other colleagues have correlated and/or the data from research projects they themselves have conducted. I wanted to ascertain what they discovered in their investigations and open my mind to other rituals, worship practices, and locations that I would otherwise have ignored. As a result I gained a profound openness to exploring a multitude of creative worship practices. For example, during my

---

[8] In the *intermezzo* "time" McGann proposes the term *kairos* as a way of articulating the intersection of God's time with human history. Her ethnographic data suggest that the community members do not see clear dichotomies between the sacred and the profane, for God is to be worshiped at all times and in all places. In the *intermezzo* "space" she develops the notion of "cosmic geography" as the "here and there touch" in ritual activity.

participant observations of Helen Rosario, I found myself participating in a Filipino devotional prayer to Mary, the Mother God,
during the month of May, otherwise known as *Flores de Mayo*.
During another event I accompanied Edward as we joined the
parish's annual "Outside Stations of the Cross" procession on
Good Friday, on the streets of the neighborhood surrounding the
parish church. On other occasions I received "text messages" on
my cell phone from the cell phone of Irene, whom I had invited to
send photos whenever she experienced a "this is church!" moment
during different social events and days of the week.

As a second set of learning objectives, I wanted to discover what
specific questions these social scientists were asking in order to
gain starting points for formulating my own set of questions. For
example, in *Everyday Religion*, Nancy Ammerman provides a
sampling of these questions, "grounded in the everyday ways
modern persons relate to the things they experience as religious or
spiritual." They include:

> What are [religion's] characteristics and dynamics?
>
> *How* does religion operate in the modern world?
>
> When and where do we find experiences that participants define as
> religious or spiritual?
>
> Where do we see symbols and assumptions that have spiritual
> dimensions, even if they are not overtly defined as such?
>
> Where are traditional religions present beyond their own institu-
> tional walls, and where are new religiosities gaining a
> foothold?[9]

I found several of these questions very useful. In response to
Ammerman's first question I discovered that some of my participants are redefining their own catholicity while others are combin-

---

[9] Nancy T. Ammerman, "Introduction: Observing Modern Religious Lives,"
3–18 in eadem, ed., *Everyday Religion: Observing Modern Religious Lives* (Oxford
and New York: Oxford University Press, 2007), at 5.

ing other religious traditions with their inherited Catholic faith. The dynamics remain fluid and often overlap with other social discourses of belonging and group identity. In response to Ammerman's last question I discovered that some of my participants have a profound reliance on the institutional church, particularly since established parishes like the one I studied have become centers and hubs for the passing on of their ethnic heritage to their children. At the other end, two of my participants hold no strong attachment to the hierarchical leadership of the church since the hierarchy's moral teachings hold no credibility in relation to their day-to-day experience of God. Their religious identity is gaining a foothold in the realized world of social justice and acts of charity. In short, the questions and lines of inquiry that these sociologists used provided another starting point for my line of ethnographic inquiry. In the end I placed their approaches in careful balance with the lines of inquiry that arose from my project.

The Interrelationship between Sunday Eucharist and Practices of Lived Religion in Ethnographic Methodology

Ethnographic theorists and practitioners often interrelate and track the various components and relevant elements of whatever subject they are studying. I had learned from various ethnographic approaches that stretched the boundaries of observable rituals. In the course of my research project I developed a specific methodology that intentionally focused on the interrelationship between Sunday eucharistic liturgies and everyday practices of religiosities and spiritualities. This entailed sharpening my participant observation skills so that I might better notice the interrelative dynamics that were at work in three types of settings: during Sunday eucharistic liturgies, during the everyday worship practices of my participants, and during the interviews I conducted with them and the other members of the parish.

I have already noted my observations about the physical portals and boundaries of St. Agnes's worship space, as well as the ritual inscriptions and transboundarying activities that were performed by members of the assembly and liturgical leaders. In addition, when I entered the homes or worship spaces of my participants

I intentionally focused on the transitional in-between spaces that seemingly marked off one area from another. At times my notes became entrées into deeper discussions about transboundarying ritual activities and the multilayered meanings behind them when placed in relationship with one another. In addition to seeing most of my participants during my regular visits to the parish on Sunday, I sat down with each one of them two to three times. I e-mailed a strategic set of questions to four participants, questions that focused on the interrelationship of Sunday Eucharist with their worship practices. These questions incorporated the terms "source" and "summit."

Particular questions emerged throughout my ethnographic interviews included: How do the subjects cultivate their ritual/spiritual lives? What metaphors do they use and what insights do they share about the interplay of participation in communal worship and the familial/communal/personal practices they embody? How do they perceive the sources and summits of their lives? How do they express this through practices of everyday religion and relate these practices to Sunday Eucharist?

The intent of my interviews was to discover how the participants came to interrelate their everyday worship practices with their experiences of eucharistic liturgy. I proceeded with this line of inquiry in two ways. The first method consisted of inviting them to share the many forms and practices that constituted their everyday worship and then asking them to compare these practices with the 10:30 AM Mass at St. Agnes. This "from-below" approach privileged their everyday practices of religiosities and/or spiritualities before proceeding to discover how they interrelated these practices with Sunday Eucharist.

My second approach, a more "from-above" technique, involved four out of the eight participants: Helen R., Rachel and Mark, and Helen A. I started with an image they each named as being the source and summit of their lives. This involved a threefold set of questions. In the first question I asked them: "Who or What is the source and summit of your life?" I left their interpretation of "source" and "summit" open-ended. After the ensuing conversation, I moved toward a second set of questions that asked them to describe how "the source and summit of their lives" came to be *expressed* in their day-to-day lives, either through activities, rituals, or worship practices: for example, "Are you *doing* or *feeling* anything particular when you become *aware* of this source or summit?" or "What does that *look* like?" Finally, I asked them how they came to interrelate their responses to my questions about Sunday Mass, and whether there were connections or disconnections between the two sets of practices. The goal of this second method was to discover how the participants came to express "associative links" between the official terms "source and summit" and their everyday practices of religiosities and spiritualities, and thus inspire my own process of rethinking the mantra, "The liturgy is the source and summit of Christian life."

Ethnographic Participants and the Interrelationship between Practices of Everyday Religiosities and Spiritualities and the 10:30 AM Eucharistic Liturgy

The narrative strands and interpretive frameworks I gleaned from my interviews, which we have read at the beginning of each chapter, will now be summarized.

Helen Rosario

For Helen, God is the source and summit of her life because God created her and provides her with "the grace to survive." Specific prayers (including Mass) and devotional practices have specific purposes. For example, her daily novena to the Infant of Prague, which begins each hour from 7:00 AM to 4:00 PM and lasts approximately five minutes each time, is prayed for the intention of her granddaughter, while "the Mass" is aimed toward the "honoring [of] God, first of all" and is an opportunity to ask for the forgiveness of her sins. While her daily devotional prayers are usually performed unilaterally, she noted the role of the priest during Mass; the priest "guides" the assembly and interprets the gospel reading. She finds this quite useful since she does not find enough time to do this herself. Finally, while she said that her personal favorite among all of her daily prayers is the Angelus (it reminds her of her grandmother), she placed no importance on one prayer over another since her image of God is of One who does not discriminate, but listens to all prayers.

Edward Williams

Edward discovered AA meetings during a time in his life when his negative experiences of "religion" led him to seek something "spiritual" and discover "the higher power." AA meetings include moments for communal prayer and are a source for spiritual nourishment and transformation. Joining AA was "the best decision" he ever made in his life. However, as he began to search for "something more" he reconnected with religion when he experienced hospitality and community at St. Agnes during their eucharistic liturgy. He returns week after week to St. Agnes, not so much "to go to Mass," but more due to his affinity with the community. He finds that the Mass has "the same spirituality" as AA, since both include prayer rituals, opportunities for spiritual transformation, and experiences with "the higher power." But even here he finds a deeper fellowship in AA since there is a more profound sense of trust fostered among its members.

Jude Penland

Jude's everyday praying of the office consists of morning, midday, and evening prayers. She uses *The Short Breviary* for midday prayer and an application on her iPad for morning and evening prayers. Her recitation of morning and midday prayer often coincides with other functions (meal blessings, drinking coffee, or taking medicine). Of the three prayers, she notes that evening prayer is more formal, because it reminds her of the first time she prayed Vespers with her Benedictine sisters in Washington. Her recitation of the Office "connects" her to the monastery, while Sunday Eucharist (remember she calls it "The Show") and her praying from *The Sacred Space* booklets during Advent and Lent connect her to community of St. Agnes. She views herself as "the string" between both communities.

Rachel Pinette and Mark Durst

For Rachel, God is the source and summit of her life and this is expressed through everyday practices of "chatting with God," meal prayers with her family, and classroom prayers, as well as through weekly Sunday Mass at St. Agnes. Sunday Mass helps her be faithful to God and reminds her of her commitment to her community. Her "chats with God," which involve mental and emotional processes that help her become aware of God's presence, are conversations, usually in silence, that take place while she is driving and doing chores. They are less formulaic than her classroom prayers, as she usually remains open to the direction they take. These chats with God also take place while she is commuting to and from St. Agnes on Sunday mornings. All these worship practices are connected to God, yet they are different experiences of the same God.

For Mark, his family is the source of his life since his family "brings [him] back" and nourishes him as nothing else does. Different everyday communication practices with his family remind him of this source, while family meal prayers are more ritualized expressions. The summit(s) of his life involve these daily links to his family, his weekly worship during Sunday Mass, and "holiday liturgies" that integrate church services and the presence of his family members.

Irene Duller and James Robinson

Neither James's nor Irene's spiritual life is contingent on whether they go to Mass at St. Agnes every week. For James, all forms of constructive and positive practices, including going to Mass, contribute to his approach to religion, God, and moral standards. For Irene any moment when and any place where she experiences "something really awesome or radical" could potentially lead to an acknowledgment of God's presence. These moments form her everyday spirituality and sometimes lead her to say out loud, "this is church!" to the people around her. "Church," as distinct from "the Mass," which she designates as occurring within a building, could be any place where she feels God's presence. These moments occur more readily in her life than "going to Mass."

Helen Chen Abrams

Helen describes her worship practices as consisting of meal prayers, Sunday Eucharist, where she serves as an acolyte and as a lector, prayers from the *Sacred Space* booklet, which she reads from her iPhone while she commutes to St. Agnes from San Mateo, and "worship through service." Of all forms of worship outside of Mass, it is this last type she identifies with most. But even here she draws a direct connection between the scriptural readings from Sunday Mass and her service to others, especially to the students from low-income families whom she teaches during the weekdays. She believes that God has given her ministerial gifts. By going to Mass she is "reset" and, through scripture readings, becomes better "anchored" to perform her daily worship practices of service. Also, when asked about the source and summit of her life, Helen responds that it is her family, consisting of her husband, mother-in-law, and father. But even here she draws a direct relationship between her family as source "on earth" and God who is the source of everything.

Correlation of Interpretations of Practices of Everyday Religiosities and Spiritualities and the 10:30 AM Eucharistic Liturgy

We have seen a variety of forms and types of worship practices, including popular devotions, AA meetings; the morning, midday, and evening prayers that make up the Office; chatting with God while driving; meal blessings; texting photos of "this is church!"; worship practices of service; and acts of social justice. By extension, the variety of practices also pointed to a variety of locations: domestic settings (kitchen, dining room, bedrooms, living room, and bathroom), church buildings, school, hospital, CalTrain, car, and even a rock concert. Almost all hours of the morning, afternoon, and evening were accounted for, with the exception of deep night, from 11:00 PM to 6:00 AM. In this final section I will correlate these interpretations into three categories: (1) types of rituals, practices, and performances; (2) how the participants described their everyday worship practices; and (3) what we can learn from

the participants and their reflections on the interrelationship between everyday worship practices and Sunday eucharistic liturgy.

Types of Rituals, Practices, and Performances

What constitute everyday practices of religiosities and spiritualities? One of the major elements that struck me from my interviews
and participant observations was the variety of ritual forms, practices, and performances that my eight participants engaged in
every day. Some used more structured prayer forms, such as Jude's
daily praying of the Office, to more casual practices, such as Irene's
spontaneous reaction to acknowledging God's presence at any
given time of the day and location. But on closer inspection, Jude's
ritual performances of morning, midday, and evening prayer demonstrate different degrees of formality. For example, her morning
prayer in the kitchen when she is still "waking up" usually accom-
panies more functional actions such as drinking coffee or taking
her medicine, while her evening prayer "after work" serves as a
"more formal" prayer ritual since it reminds her of the structured
schedule that marks the Vesper service around the same time in
Our Lady of the Rock monastery.

Another spectrum to consider is the *quantity* or *number* of worship practices the participants engage in every day. For Helen R.
every hour of the morning, afternoon, and evening is accounted
for with some form of popular devotion or eucharistic celebration,
whereas for Mark a simple meal blessing before dinner is the only
ritualized form of prayer he practices each day. The variety of
objects and tools that are used for these worship practices is worth
noting. Helen C., Irene, and Jude take advantage of modern technology devices such as iPhones and iPads, while others use prayer
booklets such as *The Sacred Space*, or the dozens of devotional
cards, statues, rosaries, and pictures that occupy every room in the
home of Helen R. These people demonstrated the use of "publicly
available symbolic forms through which [they] experience and
express meaning."[10]

---

[10] Ann Swidler, *Talk of Love: How Culture Matters* (Chicago: University of
Chicago Press, 2001), 12.

How the Participants Described Their Everyday Worship Practices

I was able to participate in and observe the everyday worship practices of four participants.[11] For the remaining participants I was dependent on my interviews. How the eight of them described their everyday worship practices was just as important as what they actually said they did. First, one of the more popular forms of communicating their thoughts and reflections about everyday worship practices was the sharing of stories. Many times when I anticipated short answers, I received longer answers that took on narrative forms and paths, consequently leading to "the unfolding of plots, characters, relationships, and motivations" that Ammerman[12] suggested. For example, Jude was always more than eager to share many stories with me: her conversion to Roman Catholicism, her first visit to the Benedictine monastery, stories about her workplace in St. Francis Hospital or Giants Stadium, etc. These stories were forever intertwined with her ritual performances of praying the Office. Her lunch breaks became opportunities for "ritual interruptions" (Ammerman) between her relationships with her co-workers and her awareness of God's presence.

For Helen R., particular devotions had particular links to stories of her teenage years in the Philippines. Praying the Angelus was not just about recalling the scriptural account of the Annunciation—in fact, when I asked her what that prayer was about, she guessed it had something to do with the Nativity—but in fact it became a portal to the cherished memory of her grandmother, who took care of her and her siblings during a difficult period in their lives. For Edward, asking him to describe AA spirituality led to stories about his whole life conversion process and how he finally found his higher power through Glide Memorial Church. His storytelling style was often marked by "contradictions, tensions,

---

[11] These included the novena to the Santo Niño with Helen R., a meal prayer during dinnertime with Mark and Rachel, and my regular reception of texts via iPhone from Irene.

[12] See n. 9 above.

and ironies" (Bartkowski)[13] as he shared how his levels of affiliation with different social groups were highly contingent upon his sense of community and fellowship. Finally, for Mark, asking him why his family is the source and summit of his life led to stories of feeling lonely during his business trips when he became disconnected with family members. His focus on "family members" clearly articulated boundary actions between his "loved ones" and the parishioners of St. Agnes Church.

Being "connected" and making connections (or sometimes disconnections) was another feature. These participants often expressed some connection with other people, communities, or groups. Edward's AA meetings are not only opportunities for spiritual transformation but also involve fellowship and levels of trust that are different from his experiences with religious institutions. At the same time, it is his experience of fellowship and community at St. Agnes that makes him maintain a connection with religion, an experience he has not encountered with other Christian denominations. For Helen R., every devotional prayer she prays becomes an opportunity to offer a petition for one of many family members. Lately, her hourly novena to the Infant of Prague is offered for her granddaughter, who is currently in high school and in need of better study skills. For Rachel and Mark, meal prayers form an important part of their family rituals. Further, the presence of family members during important liturgical feastdays forms an integral component of Mark's experience of what constitutes Sunday Eucharist. For Jude, different prayer forms connect her to different worship communities: praying the Office connects her directly to her Benedictine sisters and the Christians worldwide who regularly participate in this form of prayer, while her weekly Sunday eucharistic celebrations and prayers that pour out of an Advent/Lenten prayer booklet draw an immediate connection to her community at St. Agnes. For Helen A., her "worship of service" connects her to students from low-income families and

---

[13] See John P. Bartkowski, "Connections and Contradictions: Exploring the Complex Linkages between Faith and Family," 153–66 in *Everyday Religion*.

serves as her response to Jesus' Gospel message and the Roman Catholic tradition of social justice.

Finally, I heard expressions of feelings and emotions throughout my interviews and participant observations. In my short interviews with parishioners after Mass they frequently used the word "feel" in their responses. During my interviews with Helen R. she often punctuated her responses with "That's how I feel," as if to verify her own convictions about her faith, beliefs, and prayerful life. Jude would use the word "feel" in her descriptions of how her everyday worship practices "connected" her with her Benedictine sisters and the community of St. Agnes. She would also express excitement and joy when informing me how much she prefers specific prayers (Psalm 150 and the Magnificat) over other prayers to the point of praying these texts aloud. For Rachel, her "chats with God" were located in her "emotions," suggesting that her imaginary chats moved beyond the cognitive and toward the heart: "It's in my imagination: it's in my heart, because my heart gets engaged as well. You know, if I'm upset about something, it's not just the thoughts but the emotions as well." Mark, a mathematician, made this distinction when he spoke about spiritual nourishment: "It's not intellectual nourishment. It's just the *feeling* of experiencing, you know, loving someone and being loved in return." James described his experience of being "reset" after attending Mass as a feeling and not as an intellectual resetting of the mind, while Irene described her experiences of "this is church" as a "critical-mass type of feeling." All of this suggests that feelings and emotions form a critical component of the way the participants came to articulate, experience, and make sense of their everyday worship practices. One is reminded of Peter Phan's critique of the classical form of Vatican II's reformed rites ("*sobrietas, verevitas, simplicitas,* and linear rationality") and the accompanying need for "emotional and total involvement in liturgical celebrations."[14]

[14] Peter C. Phan, "Liturgy of Life as Summit and Source of Eucharistic Liturgy: Church Worship as Symbolization of the Liturgy of Life?" 257–78 in idem, *Being Religious Interreligiously: Asian Perspectives on Interfaith Dialogue in Postmodernity,* at 275.

What We Can Learn from My Subjects Regarding the Interrelationships between Everyday Worship Practices and Sunday Eucharistic Liturgy

I have learned the following about various everyday practices of religiosities and spiritualities, including eucharistic liturgy, and the interrelationships between them as interpreted by the eight participants.

Helen Rosario

Different worship forms have different purposes, intentions, and goals. Feelings expressed through the recalling of past memories fortify different degrees of personal favorites among a variety of worship practices. While favorite prayer forms may emerge and distinctions may be made between various everyday worship practices, including eucharistic liturgies, God, as the source and summit of one's life, may be perceived as showing no discrimination among the variety of prayer forms.

Edward Williams

While specific spiritual or religious worship rituals (e.g., the Serenity Prayer, the Our Father, and Sunday Mass) may become sources for spiritual nourishment, such rituals may not be as important as larger concerns of communal belonging. Connected to this, positive experiences of community and fellowship can motivate more participation during communal worship rituals, while negative experiences can lead to the abandonment of worship participation. God may be perceived as "the higher power" and experienced in both AA meetings and eucharistic liturgies.

Jude Penland

Worshipers may become connective "strings" to various communities of accountability during individual performances of official prayer forms (e.g., the Daily Office) and communal celebrations of official worship (e.g., eucharistic liturgies). Everyday worship practices may make use of different objects and resources, including prayer booklets and electronic readers, as aids during ritual performances. Everyday worship practices may coincide with functional activities such as drinking coffee and taking medicine, or be integrated with other prayer forms such as meal blessings.

Rachel Durst

God as source and summit may be expressed in different ways *within the same person* during individual, ecclesial, and familial worship practices and contexts. Everyday worship practices may take on different forms, from conversational mental chats that may occur during transit activities to more formulaic patterns that may occur in workplace locations (e.g., classrooms) or ecclesial settings (e.g., St. Agnes Church). Worship practices, from meal blessings to weekly eucharistic liturgies, may become opportunities for deepening one's commitments to God, family, and community.

Mark Durst

Non-theological or non-liturgical terms such as "family" may become expressions of what constitutes the source and summit of one's life. Non-worship rituals (e.g., conversations on the phone or e-mailing) *may eventually lead to* future awareness of God's presence in different religious or social contexts. Official liturgies may be directly linked to and defined by the physical presence of loved ones during holiday liturgies when family members come together to celebrate these occasions.

Irene Duller and James Robinson

One's spiritual life is not contingent upon weekly participation in official liturgies. For James, various forms of constructive and positive practices could help "reset" religious and moral standards for everyday living. For Irene the recognition of God's presence through the expression of a spiritual mantra (e.g., "this is church!") may occur during any moment in everyday life and in a number of geographical locations.

Helen Chen Abrams

Everyday worship practices may make use of different objects and resources as aids during ritual performances, including prayer booklets and electronic devices. Worship prayer forms may incorporate embodied activities of service and performances of social justice. At the same time, Sunday Eucharist, particularly the Liturgy of the Word, may become foundational "anchors" to future worship practices that lead to Christian service in everyday life. Non-theological or non-liturgical terms such as "family" may become expressions of what constitutes the source and summit of one's life. While family members may become a source of support "on earth," God may still be perceived as the source of everything.

Summary

As Mary McGann suggests, new insights, new paradigms, and new connections may be gained through the work of ethnography. Chapter 6 has interpreted and correlated the lived liturgical and worship experiences of eight members of St. Agnes Church. These nonexperts in my study demonstrate, as Robert Schreiter and the sociologists of religion propose, the complexity of worship practices that continually and inextricably become "woven through the fabric of human life." As a result they demonstrate that the official worship boundaries of St. Agnes Church remain porous, while at the same time they create new paradigms for how we may approach the interrelationship of Sunday Eucharist and the everyday worship practices of religiosities and spiritualities.

Chapter Seven

The Interrelationship of Sunday Eucharist and Everyday Practices of Religiosities and Spiritualities: Correlations and Theological Implications

I asked Jude, an oblate of the Benedictine community of Our Lady of the Rock Monastery in Shaw Island, Washington, to describe her "everyday worship life." While she only visits the monastery two to three times a year, she remains faithful to her daily recitation of the Liturgy of the Hours:[1] "I try to do at least Lauds and Vespers every day." She begins with midday prayer at noon, when she is alone in her office in the hospital. Reading from *The Short Breviary*, she sits in front of her desk, recites the prayer, which lasts about five minutes, and then proceeds to eat her lunch. "It's my way of praying grace before the meal." Most of the time she prays the Office in silence, but at other times, especially if there is a psalm or canticle she really likes (such as Psalm 150 or the

---

[1] The Liturgy of the Hours (also known as "the Office") is built upon two traditions: monastic and cathedral. The monastic tradition consists of eight time periods throughout the day —Matins ("Night Office"), Lauds (Dawn, 3:00 AM), Prime (Early Morning Prayer, First Hour, 6:00 AM), Terce (Mid-Morning Prayer, Third Hour, 9:00 AM); Sext (Midday Prayer, Sixth Hour, 12:00 PM), None (Mid-Afternoon Prayer, Ninth Hour, 3:00 PM), Vespers (Lucernarium, Evening Prayer, 6:00 PM), and Compline (Night Prayer, 9:00 PM)—while the cathedral tradition primarily centers around Morning and Evening Prayer. Jude's reference to "the Office" is to morning, midday, and evening prayers.

Magnificat), she recites the prayer out loud. Jude keeps *The Short Breviary* in her office; at home she uses her iPad and the *Universalis* application.

❖　❖　❖

In my second interview with Helen Chen Abrams, I asked her to name in a few words "the source and summit of her life," seeking to discover her associative terms. She responded: "My family . . . my husband, who is very nurturing." She explained a little bit more.

> My husband provides my emotional well-being. My mother-in-law is . . . very kind, non-judgmental, and my dad is very logical, good to talk with, especially for problem solving. These have been the sources of my life . . . I would like to think that despite the lack of religious belief on the part of my husband, father, and mother-in-law, God is still providing me support through tough times by working *through* these agents. I start to feel very blessed because I have such emotional support and all these come from God. Everything I have that is good, I feel, is thanks to God. So I would say my family is the source when I think of my immediate answer . . . but if I dig deeper, I believe that my source "on earth" is a gift from God. *I think everything comes from God!*

❖　❖　❖

In chapter 2 I argued that throughout the span of the liturgical movement certain ecclesial leaders and liturgical scholars, in their concern to relate official liturgy with Christian life, used the image of the liturgy as source and summit in order to promote more lay participation during official liturgy and to reorder the relationship between Eucharist and popular religious practices. But as the movement progressed, their vigorous promotion of the Eucharist also led to a decreased promotion of popular religious practices. In chapter 3 I presented two documents from the Second Vatican Council and some of the writings of John Paul II and Benedict XVI to demonstrate how these writings maintained a hierarchical reordering between official liturgy and all other non-official worship practices and further solidified the image of the Eucharist as source and summit. But, throughout this process of reordering and solidification, the fluidity of interactions between official liturgy and non-official worship practices remained.

In chapter 4 I argued that Peter Phan's theological paradigm does not narrow the contextual horizon of liturgical scholarship to eucharistic liturgies alone but, instead, broadens the scope and spectrum of what constitutes "liturgy" by borrowing Karl Rahner's "liturgy of the world," renaming it "the liturgy of life," and proposing that the liturgy of life is the summit and source of the official liturgy and popular religion and, further, that both of these worship practices together constitute the one worship that humanity renders to God. In chapter 5 I explored and analyzed the writings of sociologists of religion in order to uncover the pluriform practices of worship that occur in everyday life. Their scientific approaches to religious practices advanced the goal of this book by providing methodological tools for my own ethnographic fieldwork. The presentation of that fieldwork formed the basis for chapters 1 and 6, in which I argued how the ethnographic study of one Roman Catholic worship community in San Francisco, including the worship experiences and practices of eight members of this community, provides useful interpretive data on how Christians interrelate Sunday Eucharist with all other non-official worship practices.

The purpose of this final chapter is to argue that an interdisciplinary conversation among the three perspectives of this book (theological, sociological, and ethnographic) confirms, stretches, and recontextualizes the theological framework I have drawn from Phan regarding the liturgy of life, and that the goals I set out for my study have significant implications for the field of liturgical studies. First I will correlate the information and content from the preceding chapters further. Specifically, I will place the interpretive data I have gleaned from my ethnographic research project in conversation with the historical strands that emerged from chapters 2 and 3, Phan's proposal of the liturgy of life in chapter 4, and the writings of the sociologists of religion we examined in chapter 5. Then I will attempt to show how this study contributes to the current effort to retrieve the divine initiative in the field of liturgical theology. For the past ten years liturgical scholars Kevin W. Irwin and Michael B. Aune have suggested that focus on ecclesial and pastoral concerns in the field of liturgical theology since the Second Vatican Council has led to a neglect of a more serious consideration of God's divine action. As I will show, the work behind this book not only aligns with and complements their concerns but also stretches this conversation to a new liturgical-theological paradigm.

Correlation of Theological, Sociological, and Ethnographic Findings

In the previous chapter we learned that non-experts also interrelate various forms of worship practices in their everyday lives and, at times, develop and sustain their own degrees of reordering of their worship practices. Evidence of significant interrelationships between worship practices appeared from that project. Three such interrelationships emerged in my assessment: (1) communal and emotionally embodied links between worship forms, (2) the integration of functional needs (including the use of cultural products) and the creation of hybrid prayer forms during the ritual performances of everyday worship practices, (3) the expansion of ecclesial worship boundaries as a result of interrelating worship practices. These yielded a basis for the expansion of academic inquiry into the liturgy of life through interrelating associative terms for source and summit by non-experts.

Correlation One: Communal and Emotionally Embodied Links between Worship Forms

Jude's official worship practices consist of praying the Office every day (morning, midday, and evening) and participating regularly at Sunday Mass. Her worship repertoire demonstrates that worshipers can ritually embody the linkages between a variety of communal affiliations and accountabilities. She continually negotiates the number of times a day she prays the Office and participates at Mass, but her commitment to pray Morning Prayer is not as strong as her commitment to Evening Prayer, and the frequency with which she prays the Office, in the nature of the case, surpasses that of her participation at Sunday Mass. With each commitment to perform a prayer there is an opportunity to connect with a group of other worshipers. This is closely tied to Edward's observation when my line of inquiry, which focused on "the Mass" as an official event, did not resonate with his main reason for "going to Mass" and remaining a member of the St. Agnes community: it was the initial contact with a Jesuit priest during an AA meeting that drew him to St. Agnes, and the deeply felt community and fellowship that he first experienced within the hospitality area of the church continually reaffirmed his decision to participate regularly during Sunday Mass, not the other way around.

As noted in the previous chapter, the participants in my project shared these experiences with me mainly through stories of people and group affiliations, often displaying different ranges of human emotions. During my participant observations of the annual *Flores de Mayo* devotion, which was celebrated by twenty-four members of the Filipino Ministry Group (including Helen R.) on a Sunday morning right before the 10:30 AM Mass, I noticed that the eyes of several worshipers would brim with tears during the recitation of the rosary; their affiliation with the group provided a safe environment for the display of feelings and emotions. When the praying of the rosary ended around 10:20 AM, a procession began. That procession, led by a statue of Mary that was placed atop a small platform and held up by four people, circled around the parking lot, moved along the sidewalk around the church, and made its way through the front doors of the church; eventually the participants became "the lead ministers" for the opening procession at Mass, for which the larger St. Agnes community had already gathered. By that time the emotional atmosphere had shifted from quiet tear-filled eyes to one marked by jubilation, joy, and smiles.

These examples of interrelating worship practices demonstrate one of the reasons why I chose to pursue an ethnographic component to this book: namely, the official documents and the writings of liturgical theologians examined throughout chapters 1–3 focused on prayer *forms*, theological doctrine, and/or ritual prescriptions in their attempts to interrelate worship practices. What remained missing in these past approaches were descriptions of the heartfelt rituals and emotionally embodied sensibilities and negotiations by the worshipers themselves and how these sensibilities and negotiations influenced what constituted worship for them.

Johann Adam Möhler's doctrine of the Mystical Body of Christ became a theological thread throughout the nineteenth and twentieth centuries by providing a critical imagery for understanding *the ecclesial body* of the church during official worship practices. But the development of that doctrine, which culminated in 1943 in Pius XII's encyclical, *Mystici Corporis Christi*, continually clashed with the hierarchy's suspicious stance toward the expression (the embodiment) of emotions during popular religious practices. The roots of that stance could be traced back to nineteenth-century Romanizing efforts at controlling these practices. As Peter Phan has argued, these suspicious attitudes challenged post–Vatican II efforts to reappropriate the dialogue between official liturgy and popular piety. What I have learned from my ethnographic project is that ritual forms, official or non-official, that accent and foster communal and emotionally embodied links between persons and communities can be potential starting points for accessing and reflecting upon the interrelationship of worship forms.

Correlation Two: The Integration of Functional Needs (Including the Use of Cultural Products) and the Creation of Hybrid Prayer Forms during the Ritual Performances of Everyday Worship Practices

In the everyday worship practices of Jude and Rachel we learn that some practices coincide with functional (often mundane) activities. Jude's reluctance at times to perform her morning prayer as often as her evening prayer is largely due to the time of day: her daily routine is initiated by her cats, who wake her to be fed. She admitted that this form of prayer often coincides with her morning routines of drinking coffee and taking her medicine. For Rachel, her everyday worship practice of chatting with God takes place during the functional activity of driving her car, and often while she performs daily chores. Sometimes these practices blend into official worship practice when she engages in these chats on her way to Sunday Mass or reflects upon the Mass while driving home. The line between "worship practice" and "functional practice" becomes more blurred during these moments. Sometimes the combining of worship practices leads to hybrid forms of prayer, as in the case of Jude's praying of Midday Prayer (*official* worship), which simultaneously serves as a meal blessing for the lunch that is laid before her.

In the official documents and writings investigated in chapters 1 and 2, consideration of *legitimizing* hybrid worship forms remained for the most part nonexistent, primarily due to the efforts of the pioneers of the liturgical movement to demarcate popular religious practices from official worship. (At that time it was not uncommon for worshipers to engage in popular devotions *during* eucharistic liturgies). The efforts on the part of the pioneers to differentiate official from non-official worship practices is a testament to this, as is the solidification that placed the Eucharist "on top" of the worship pyramid. It was not until a consideration of the insights of Peter Phan, Mark Francis, and James Empereur that questions of the legitimization of hybrid forms between official worship and popular piety emerged in my study. This was illustrated by Empereur's observation of the "strange anomalies" one encounters when considering current official worship practices, including the inclusion of the Advent wreath during Sunday Eucharist and the celebration of Divine Mercy Sunday on the Second Sunday of Easter. Recall Francis's observation that more historical studies demonstrating how worshipers *have always* combined different prayers forms are needed.

In comparing the everyday worship practices by Jude, Helen A., and Irene, we learned that worshipers often make use of cultural products, such as electronic devices or prayerbooks as worship aids during ritual performances. These included the Advent and Lenten prayer booklets, *The Sacred Ground*, used by Jude and Helen A., an iPad for morning and evening prayers used by Jude, and an iPhone by Irene (at my suggestion). What we learn from Jude, Helen A., and Irene is that technological "gadgets" used during the performance of worship rituals are also used for other non-worship practices, such as making phone calls and using other applications.

This does not assume that there was no concern about the use of cultural products during the liturgical movement, or that worshipers' use of technology is only a contemporary phenomenon and has not been investigated by liturgical theologians.[2] My point is that these products may contribute to the dialogue between official and non-official worship practices since the products themselves, as well as the worshipers who use them, cross boundaries between designated social domains (a hospital office, the inside of a train, a sidewalk in downtown Chicago) as they also interact with one another.

Correlation Three: The Expansion of Ecclesial Worship Boundaries as a Result of Interrelating Worship Practices

Among the many interrelationships of worship practices that emerged from my study, there were two that particularly illustrate how such practices expand perceived ecclesial boundaries. The first supports what has already been written about the relationship between liturgy and social justice, while the second challenges established ecclesial boundaries of what constitute official worship practices.

First, for Helen A. the eucharistic liturgy became a source for her worship practices that involved acts of social justice, that is, the Sunday Eucharist, particularly the Liturgy of the Word, became a foundational "anchor" for future worship in the form of Christian service: "my way of worshiping is to be what Jesus would want us to be." This is seen in her choice to teach students from low-income families. Mass "resets" her sense of being "distracted" from Jesus' commandment to serve, and her worship there, in turn, draws her "closer to God" in everyday life. Interestingly, the term "reset" also arose in James's description of Mass to provide "a clean slate" that

---

[2] For an historical survey of Christians' use of worship aids, see Edward Foley, *From Age to Age: How Christians Have Celebrated the Eucharist: Revised and Expanded Edition* (Chicago: Liturgy Training Publications, 2008). For the historic development of the use of modern technological products during worship, see Eileen D. Crowley, *Liturgical Art for a Media Culture* (Collegeville, MN: The Liturgical Press, 2007).

later leads to prayers of thanksgiving and reminders of how he is called to "take care" of people. When I asked Helen if she was familiar with Catholic teachings on social justice, she affirmed my observation. Helen's practices of social justice and James's approach to Mass as "resetting" his moral conscious reveal striking parallels with the interplay between official worship and the writings of the American liturgical pioneers during the liturgical movement. One recalls Virgil Michel's vision of how participation during official liturgies ought to lead to participation in social activism and how Michel found inspiration for this vision not only in official documents (most notably Leo XIII's *Rerum Novarum* of 1891), but also Möhler's theology of the Mystical Body of Christ.

These interwoven strands of liturgy and social justice were confirmed officially through later documents, including Pius XII's encyclicals, *Mystici Corporis Christi* (1943) and *Mediator Dei* (1947), Vatican II's Dogmatic Constitution on the Church (1964) with its concern for the interrelationship between the Eucharist and "the whole Christian life," and the writings of Pope John Paul II, particularly articles 69–72 of his 1998 *Dies Domini*, and Benedict XVI's *Sacramentum Caritatis* (2007). An interplay thus emerges among official worship, Helen's "worship through service" (her term), James's "resetting" of moral consciousness, and the link between the social teaching and the ecclesial identity of the church.

The second example of how the interrelationship of worship practices expands ecclesial worship boundaries comes from Irene's practice of recognizing God's presence through the expression of her spiritual mantra, "This is church!" This occurred during different moments of daily life and in a number of geographical locations. Irene's use of the term "church" as a way to designate God's ongoing universal presence in the world moves beyond the official criterion that defined "church" as "the House of God"/"The Temple" (from Pius X's *Tra le Sollecitudini*, 1903) or, in this case, the building of St. Agnes Church. Indeed, Irene's experiences of "church" are, as Karl Rahner believed, explicit interruptions, acknowledging God's grace in the mundane context of everyday life. These are mystical encounters that involve a "searching out" of the "hidden experience of the abiding, absolute mystery of God." As Michael Skelley explains, "While God is always present to us, some events refer us more clearly than others to the incomprehensible mystery that surrounds us."[3] At the same time, Irene's awareness during these moments, accompanied by her mantra, extends the boundaries of what constitutes popular religion or popular piety. One is challenged to label these worship practices into any clear-cut category, as Empereur and Francis argue.

Finally, Irene and James's less frequent practice of attending Sunday Mass converges with many of the conclusions by the sociologists of religion. For Irene and James, the starting point of their experiences of worship is located *outside* of official worship, as well as beyond official expectations of accountability such as the church's obligation in the Sunday Eucharist; micro-level practices of everyday worship were negotiated, at times, with their interpretations of macro-level institutional requirements. There is interplay between the terms "spirituality" and "religion": while both Irene and James use the term "spirituality" to describe their everyday worship practices, some of these, most notably Irene's mantra, "this is church," have clear links to metaphors that stem from religious institutions and traditions. Hence, Irene borrows terms such as "church," or ritual practices such as "lighting candles," as a means to negotiate between the micro- and macro-levels of her everyday worship practices.

Correlative Result: Academic Inquiry into the Liturgy of Life as Source and Summit

During my ethnographic inquiry I considered how some of the participants associated the terms "source and summit" with their everyday worship practices and Sunday Mass. Some qualifications remain in order. Although it would be unfair to evaluate my participants' responses to these questions with the same academic criteria as those applied to official statements and the writings of liturgical theologians, I have demonstrated that the phrase "source and summit" has been used as an overarching term and metaphor

---

[3] Michael Skelley, *The Liturgy of the World: Karl Rahner's Theology of Worship* (Collegeville, MN: Liturgical Press, 1991), 80.

to articulate the relationship and interplay between official liturgy, especially the Eucharist, and all other activities of Christian life. Having established this, I wanted to discover what non-experts associated with these popularly used terms so often used in theological discourse. My aim was not to pit written discourse by theological experts against the articulations of non-experts—after all, some of what the participants interpreted as worship probably would never qualify as "official worship"—but use their responses to stretch my own imagination and develop conceptual tools to articulate how their experiences and associations might inform and even expand present day inquiry on this subject. Furthermore, what we can learn from their answers could influence the pastoral implementation of practices interrelating official and non-official forms of worship.

First, I discovered many correlations between Helen R.'s worship practices (mainly consisting of popular devotions and eucharistic liturgies) and Phan's examples of the relationship between the liturgy of life and popular religion. Most intriguing was Helen's response to my question: "So how would you *compare* praying the Angelus to going to daily Mass?" I purposely chose the word "compare" rather than leading her toward a hierarchical ranking of her prayer forms, in order to remain open to her response: "*They are all the same to me*, meaning to say that God is listening to what I'm asking for." When I asked her "Who or What is the source of your life?" she gave me a one-word answer, "God." The interrelationship of these responses with her earlier admission that the Angelus remains her "personal favorite" demonstrates that Helen perceives no systematic reordering or "ranking" of prayer forms *from the side of God*, but there may remain personal favorites *from the side of the worshiper*. In short, "God does not discriminate" (Helen's words!); humans do.

From the start of the liturgical movement through the postconciliar documents of Vatican II, the interrelationship between official liturgy, popular religious practices, and Christian life was one of the chief concerns of ecclesial leaders and liturgical scholars. At the same time, the gradual reordering and solidifying mirrored the perceived need for hierarchical control of all forms of worship practices. My point here is not to dismiss what has been achieved with regard to the central role of eucharistic practices in the life of Christians, especially since, as Phan observed, "Sunday Masses are the focal point around which the life of the parish revolves."[4] After all, each ecclesial leader and liturgical scholar was writing within a particular historical period and with a particular agenda in response to the spirit of the larger liturgical movement. Helen's interrelationship of worship practices reveals that such hierarchical considerations could benefit by being placed in dialogue with the *lived* religious and spiritual experiences and interpretations that stem from the worshipers themselves: non-experts who daily and sometimes hourly, as in Helen's example, live out their entire life in prayerful worship and devotion to God.

Among all the participants, I found Rachel's systematic approach to interrelating her worship practices to be more thought out than those of the other participants, perhaps because she teaches religion in a high school. To this extent she may be regarded as a "theological expert." She explained how her "three experiences of God as source" came to be expressed through three types of worship practices: the "God of . . . personal prayer" was expressed through her "chats with God" while driving in the car, "the God of . . . church community" was expressed in her participation during Sunday Eucharist at St. Agnes, and "the God of . . . family" was expressed in her meal prayers with her family and her prayers with her students in the classroom. There were moments when these practices crossed common boundaries. For example, her chats with God in the car not only took place during her daily routine but sometimes during her actual commutes to and from St. Agnes Church, particularly when she found herself driving alone across the Bay Bridge. While there was no strong effort on her part to reorder these practices by placing one "above" another, in general she saw the value of each practice as demonstrative of her belief that God

[4] Peter Phan, "Liturgy of Life as Summit and Source of Eucharistic Liturgy: Church Worship as Symbolization of the Liturgy of Life?" 257–78 in idem, *Being Religious Interreligiously: Asian Perspectives on Interfaith Dialogue in Postmodernity*, at 261.

was the source of each and all of them and thus revealed a level of convergence with Phan's proposal of the liturgy of life: that is, the Eucharist and popular religious practices together constitute the one worship humanity renders to God. But even here we run into the same terminological difficulties noted above: how does one "label" personal chats with God that take place while *en route* to Mass? Nevertheless, Rachel's everyday worship experiences introduce the possibility (or belief?) that God as source and summit may be expressed through different rituals and prayer forms, *sometimes within the same person*, and that the worship context—the inside of a car, the ecclesial setting of a church building, the domestic setting around a dinner table, or the workplace setting of a classroom—plays an important role during such practices.

The State of Liturgical Theology and the Delicate Balance between the Divine Initiative and the Expanding Contextual Boundaries of Worship Practices

In the previous section I demonstrated that the contextual and ecclesial boundaries of Sunday Eucharist expand when one considers the dynamic interactions that occur between official worship and everyday worship practices. In this section I will present what I have learned from this project and demonstrate how these results complement and align with a current concern about the primacy of the divine initiative in liturgical theology, that is, how liturgical scholars, in their reflection on what liturgical events mean theologically, maintain *the primacy of God acting* upon the assembly during worship rather than placing more emphasis on *what the assembly does*. Then I will offer my thoughts on the direction I believe liturgical studies could move and offer some suggestions.

In his 2003 assessment of the liturgical reforms that had emerged since the Second Vatican Council (on the occasion of the fortieth anniversary of SC), Kevin Irwin expressed concern that continuing to reflect on the divine initiative in liturgical scholarship remains one of the more critical issues liturgical theologians face today:

If one were to contrast the past forty years of liturgical change and evolution with the previous four hundred years, one could legitimately say that we have more recently been self-conscious about liturgy; what to say and do and how to enact it. This is all legitimate; in fact, it has been required by the reform of the liturgy. But I do wonder whether this aspect of liturgical engagement should have run its course by now and whether we ought not to focus on the kind of deeper liturgical renewal in spirituality, catechesis, and theology. . . . In the end, liturgy is primarily about what God does among us and for us. All that we do in liturgy is but a response to the over-arching, grace filled initiative of God. I sometimes also wonder whether emphasizing what "we do" in the liturgy is a particularly American phenomenon and preoccupation.

There is a delicate balance in liturgy: divine initiative and human response, the action of God and the sanctification of humanity. How one "achieves" this is part and parcel of liturgy as an art and a craft. . . . But even then it is not about what *we* achieve but what God works among us and through us.[5]

Four years later Michael Aune rearticulated Irwin's concern in his own assessment of the state of liturgical theology. Agreeing with Irwin that the field of liturgical theology needs "to recover once again an awareness of God's initiative, the divine action in liturgy—what God does among us and for us," Aune writes that "awareness" of divine action in liturgy "has been all but lost or certainly overshadowed in the nearly endless emphasis on church, assembly, etc."[6] Aune sharply critiques the liturgical scholarship he calls "The Schmemann-Kavanagh-Fagerberg-Lathrop line of liturgical theology." He writes that Alexander Schmemann, in seeking to

[5] Kevin W. Irwin, "A Spirited Community Encounters Christ: Liturgical and Sacramental Theology and Practice," 95–122 in *Catholic Theology Facing the Future: Historical Perspectives*, ed. Dermot A. Lane (Mahwah, NJ: Paulist Press, 2003), at 119–20. Irwin includes these observations in his more recent assessment of the liturgical reforms of Vatican II, in light of the fiftieth anniversary of the promulgation of SC. See his *What We Have Done, What We Have Failed to Do* (Mahwah, NJ: Paulist Press, 2013).

[6] Michael B. Aune, "Liturgy and Theology: Rethinking the Relationship—Part 1, Setting the Stage," *Worship* 81 (2007): 46–68, at 47.

articulate the relationship between worship and theology, placed emphasis on the *ecclesial context of liturgy* as a starting point, eclipsing the primacy of God's action.[7] From the 1980s through the 1990s liturgical scholars such as Aidan Kavanagh,[8] David Fagerberg,[9] and Gordon Lathrop[10] continued this line of thinking: "All in one way or another have contributed to an understanding of liturgy that takes its bearings from 'church,' 'assembly'—in short, the 'we' of those celebrating/worshiping. . . . This has been a constant theme in much of the liturgical-theological reflection of the past generation."[11]

Thus, Aune's thesis is:

> "liturgical theology" needs to be both more *historical* and more *theological* in its content and character, thus requiring a rethinking of how we regard the liturgy-theology relationship. What will it mean to take more seriously the "fruits of historical research"? And, what will be involved in clarifying and then deepening our experience and understanding of the "overarching, grace-filled initiative of God"?[12]

To prove his thesis, Aune moves through some of the major writings of the aforementioned theologians and critiques their conclusions through the lens of more recent historical research,[13] and then

---

[7] Aune cites Alexander Schmemann, *Introduction to Liturgical Theology* (London: Faith Press, 1966).

[8] Aune refers to Aidan Kavanagh, *On Liturgical Theology* (New York: Pueblo, 1984).

[9] The reference is to David Fagerberg, *Theologia Prima: What Is Liturgical Theology?* (Collegeville, MN: Liturgical Press, 1992).

[10] Aune cites Gordon Lathrop, *Holy Things: A Liturgical Theology* (Minneapolis: Fortress Press, 1993).

[11] "Liturgy and Theology," 50.

[12] Ibid., 47–48.

[13] For example, Aune critiques the historical research on which Schmemann's theological synthesis rested, writing (p. 51) that "the sort of unity and synthesis in theology, worship, and life that Schmemann believed to be exemplified in the patristic period simply did not exist." As Paul F. Bradshaw has proven a number of times, there were variant liturgical traditions during the

from the perspective of a more intentional focus on God's action during worship.[14] He ends his critique on the state of liturgical theology by naming two popular theological trends that have contributed to the line of liturgical-theological thinking he is criticizing: (1) the problem of the term *leitourgia* ("liturgy") as the starting point, and (2) the continued misuse and abuse of Prosper of Aquitaine's famous phrase, *legem credendi lex statuat supplicandi*.[15] First, the oft-cited definition of the term *leitourgia* as "the work *of the people*" leads to "an emphasis on human action as the primary dynamic of this event." Aune admits that liturgy involves "something that believers *do*," but "this does not justify a wholesale theological shift from God's action to the worshiping community's action."[16] Finally, Prosper's *legem credendi lex statuat supplicandi*

---

first three centuries of Christian worship. Thus efforts on the part of some liturgical theologians to hold up this time period as paradigmatic of liturgical praxis need to be qualified by acknowledging *which tradition* is being espoused. Aune here refers to Bradshaw, *The Search for the Origins of Christian Worship*, 2d ed. (Oxford: Oxford University Press, 2002).

[14] Here he critiques Kavanagh's assertion of liturgy as "*theologia prima*," that is, the view that the worship of the church remains the "premier theological act of a community of faith, [that] it is in the act of worship that the community's primary theology is to be found" (p. 52). Such theological assertions, Aune writes, are really an exercise in "romanticism and reductionism" or, again quoting Bradshaw, presume that "when believers come to worship on a Sunday morning, they . . . come with their minds a *tabula rasa*." On the contrary, worshipers *bring into liturgical celebrations* "their religious attitudes and expectations already formed by secondary theology, as a result of the catechesis that their particular ecclesiastical tradition has given to them over the years" (p. 53, citing Bradshaw, *Search*, 191). Referring to the work of Paul V. Marshall, Aune writes that "primary theological moments may occur before or outside of participation in liturgy" (p. 53, quoting Marshall, "Reconsidering 'Liturgical Theology': Is There a *Lex Orandi* for All Christians?" *Studia Liturgica* 25 [1995]: 129–51).

[15] The original Latin phrase, *ut legem credendi lex statuat supplicandi*, is usually further condensed to *lex orandi, lex credendi* ("the law of prayer grounds the law of belief") in popular liturgical parlance. See Kevin Irwin, "*Lex Orandi, Lex Credendi*—Origins and Meaning: State of the Question," *Liturgical Ministry* 11 (Spring 2002): 57–69.

[16] "Liturgy and Theology," 64.

continues to be misused and abused as a way to justify liturgy as "a 'source' for theology," that is, that "theology's source . . . is the church's *lex orandi* [the law of prayer] which manifests an eschatological, ecclesial, and cosmological vision of Christianity."[17] Instead, liturgical theologians need to return to the historical context (i.e., "better history") in order to unveil the original intention behind Prosper's adage: it was not to place more emphasis on the church's worship life over and above the faith life of the church, but rather to emphasize the need for God's grace.[18]

While Aune provides a marvelous summary of current critical resources, my concern is that his call for better use of *historical method* and of *theological content* as a means to maintain the divine initiative within liturgical-theological reflection might eclipse consideration for the widening contextual horizon of liturgical practice. I am not saying that he dismisses this concern, but he clearly expresses a cautionary stance toward giving any more attention to the ecclesial context of liturgical events, since focus on "what we do" during liturgy has led to this present dilemma.

One of the hallmarks of Phan's proposal, namely, that "the liturgy of life and the liturgy of the church constitute the one worship that humanity renders to God and whose center and supreme fulfillment is Jesus Christ," is that it better articulates and more directly maintains the divine initiative during acts of official and non-official worship than the phrase "the Eucharist is the source and summit of Christian life." In the liturgy of life, God is viewed as *The Source* from whom all Christian life and activity flows and *The Cumulative Point* toward which all Christian life and activity returns. Recall that the articulation of how God was source and summit was one of the four points of resistance and debate during

[17] Ibid., 66.

[18] Aune writes: "According to Paul Marshall, Prosper's purpose, then, 'was to show that among his many other arguments, the universal practice of praying for people to come to believe is further evidence in support of his contention that belief is a gift.' In addition, Prosper's citation of the specific prayers was to 'further illustrate his contention about the process of coming to believe.'" "Liturgy and Theology," 67, quoting Marshall, "Reconsidering," 142.

the Second Vatican Council.[19] Yet a careful reading of the last sentence of article 10, as Phan demonstrates, reveals that *all* activities of the church are directed toward the sanctification of humanity and the glorification of God ("as toward their end").

In light of the research I have presented, one could even argue that the official and popular use of the phrase, "the Eucharist is the source and summit of Christian life," may have contributed to inordinate emphasis on the assembly's action over and above God's action in liturgy. The official articulation that "the liturgy, especially the Eucharist, is source and summit" aligns with Aune's concern about how popular terminologies (e.g., *lex orandi, lex credendi; theologia prima,* and so on) may draw our attention away from more constructive approaches to liturgical theology that considers divine initiative. But Aune's choice not to consider the contextual within his schema—or to place the contextual in dialectical partnership with the historical and the theological—leaves out of the picture the need for a re-balancing of these relationships.

It is my assertion that the contextual field upon which official and non-official worship practices transpire will always need to be considered seriously and placed in continuous dialogue with the historical and the theological, for two reasons. First, the call to utilize tools from the social sciences and to consider the cultural context of liturgical practice remains faithful to the pastoral vision of the Second Vatican Council. As Mary McGann has noted, the use of interpretive tools for liturgical scholarship flows from the Second Vatican Council's embrace of liturgical pluralism in order to better articulate "the particularity of each community's worship experience."[20] One hopes that too much attention to the theological and the historical without consideration of the contextual does not "trip the balance." Irwin writes: "at the outset that liturgy is always paschal and always pastoral—the church's central action of salvation and sanctification. Let me conclude by saying that liturgy is

[19] See above, chapter 4, p. 86.

[20] Mary E. McGann, *A Precious Fountain: Music in the Worship of an African American Catholic Community* (Collegeville, MN: Liturgical Press, 2004), xvi–xvii.

both something that *we* do and something that *does us*. We trip this balance at our peril."[21]

Second, as long as liturgical scholarship exists and liturgical theologians continue to reflect theologically upon the liturgy there will always be a need to qualify the cultural assumptions and contextual locations of each scholar. The solidification of liturgy and the Eucharist as the source and summit of Christian life has largely been a Western enterprise. One of the goals of my study was to explore the worship experiences of non-experts in order to gain deeper insights into their own interpretations of Sunday Eucharist and non-official worship practices. Because the demographic backgrounds of the participants represented a cross-section of race, gender, sexual orientation, age, and ethnicity, the interpretive data that emerged became a richer and deeper reservoir from which to correlate the theological and the historical components that appeared. What this book has demonstrated is that dialogue with the social sciences, including the call to consider more intentionally the expanding sociocultural context of worship by means of sociological and ethnographic tools, can not only lead to new paradigms to help understand *what* liturgy is and *how* liturgy is performed, but to do so while maintaining the divine initiative.

To illustrate this, I recall Edward Williams's use of the term "the higher power," during my ethnographic interviews with him. Edward's use of this term in his description of AA meetings and in eucharistic liturgies triggered my own imagination to rethink the mantra, "The Eucharist is the source and summit of Christian life." In Edward's interrelationship of worship practices we learned that one may have *more than one title* for "God." Thus I began to wonder whether "God" in the phrase "God is source and summit of Christian life" might be expressed in more than one term, title, or metaphor, in addition to the word "God," while maintaining the divine initiative of God's action during eucharistic liturgy. Edward later explained: "In AA 'higher power' is rather a generic term for 'God as you understand him,' which allows as many

---

[21] Irwin, "A Spirited Community Encounters Christ," 120.

people as possible to join the program without [its] having any religious connotations."

Edward's belief that one may have more than one title for "God" may be one key to extending Phan's assertion of the liturgy of life while still remaining faithful to his proposal that God is the source and summit of Christian life and that the Eucharist, popular devotions, and other forms of worship and spiritual practices could be *potential* expressions of the liturgy of life that, together, constitute the one worship humanity renders to God. Perhaps the task before us, then, is not to continue explorations of how "the Eucharist" *per se* is the source and summit of Christian life—or, to borrow Aune's similar stance toward *lex orandi, lex credendi*, "it may be time to either demythologize this phrase or send it into retirement"—but, rather, to explore *the many terms, titles, and metaphors* by which worshipers come to name "God" as source and summit, while still holding to the importance and dignity of Sunday Eucharist in the worshiping life of a community.

Our theological reflections on liturgy may retain acknowledgment of God's grace and initiative as the source and summit of all worship activities while remaining open to the multitude of ways by which people come to express the name of God. These could include terms such as "God," "Christ," "the higher power," and so forth, but not disregard the possibility that "the Eucharist" may be expressed as the source and summit of the worship experience of some people. After all, for Mark there is *an intimate connection* between his "family" as source and summit and the annual celebrations of the Eucharist during holidays. For Helen A. there are *two* answers to this question that form one juxtaposition: while her family serves as "the source" of her everyday lived experience as a Christian "on earth," she still maintains that God is the source of her whole life. In my estimation, Helen's response resonates more with the official phrase "the liturgy is the source and summit of Christian life" in that she juxtaposes two images as her source and summit, family and God, just as official documents have, as we have seen, juxtaposed a multitude of images for "source and summit."

Church leaders and liturgical scholars throughout the liturgical movement used the metaphors of source and summit in their careful attempts to interrelate official liturgy with the activities that mark Christian life, especially Sunday Eucharist and popular religion. While official pronouncements that sought to reorder these relationships "peaked" during the Second Vatican Council with article 10 of SC and article 11 of LG, previous documents (e.g., Leo XIII's MC and Pius XII's *MCC*) still named "Christ" as source. Postconciliar reflections by Popes John Paul II and Benedict XVI continued to maintain and even solidify the Eucharist as source and summit above all other worship practices, while simultaneously stating that Christ is the source of Christian life. Yet, despite these attempts to juxtapose the metaphor "the Eucharist as source and summit" with "Christ as source and summit" (all of which paralleled the juxtapositions between official and non-official worship practices), Peter Phan's proposal of the liturgy of life remains the most convincing and comprehensive theological assessment for how we can acknowledge the divine initiative within the scope and spectrum of all official and non-official worship practices. He achieves this *via* Rahner by naming the liturgy of life, rather than the Eucharist, as the primary metaphor for *all forms* of everyday worship practices, while maintaining and clearly articulating *the primacy of God* as the source and summit of Christian life. Further, his explanation of symbolization *as theological linkage* between all forms of worship is capable of maintaining the distinctiveness found in each form while allowing these forms to point toward the liturgy of life.

However, the results of my ethnographic project move beyond Phan's proposal by considering more extensively the many sociocultural expressions of God that confirm and stretch the theological truism of divine initiative and by examining the interrelational dynamics that exist between these expressions. Theological reflections and frameworks that take these interrelational dynamics into account could be exceptionally helpful to pastoral ministry and lead to other articulations and variations of "source and summit" that are capable of maintaining the primacy of God's divine action:

> *God*, as experienced and expressed in the eucharistic liturgy that
> takes place within communal settings, *is the source and summit of
> Christian life.*

> *God*, as experienced and expressed during the everyday worship
> practices of the liturgy of life, *is the source and summit of Christian
> life.*

> *The higher power* [i.e., God], as experienced and expressed during the
> spiritual and communal components of AA meetings and
> Sunday Eucharist, *is the source and summit of Christian life.*

> *God*, as experienced and expressed during celebrations of the Eucha-
> rist in the immediate presence of family members, *is the source
> and summit of Christian life.*

The chief metaphor that emerges from these worship experiences
remains the liturgy of life, a liturgy whose scope and spectrum of
interactional worship activities communally and officially centers
around the Eucharistic liturgy and whose end goal is the sanctification of humanity and the glorification of God. It consists of our
individual and communal grace-filled responses to the spectrum of
mystical experiences of everyday life, experiences that are initiated
by God, who continually invites us to deepen our relationship with
the Triune God and with one another.

Further, I agree with Michael Aune that better use of historical
method remains important. In fact, I would advocate for more
research in the area of historical ethnography. Perhaps future
research projects could include how engaged Christians practiced
their lived religion during the liturgical movement and not just in
contemporary times as demonstrated by my project. In her recent
volume, *There Were Also Many Women There*, Katharine Harmon
examined the role and scholarly contribution of women within
domestic settings during the liturgical movement in the United
States. She wrote:

> Rather than a realm to which women were confined, an evaluation of
> "living the liturgical life" from the perspective of the mother/wife
> reveals careful theological reflection on this vocation in the lay
> apostolate as an authentic realization of the Christian life, revealing

the degree of volition with which lay women sought to unite their roles as wife and mother with that of the liturgical apostolate.[22]

How might historical studies like this complement the writings and visions I had addressed in chapters 2 and 3, and how can more studies contribute to an ongoing dialogue that seeks to interrelate official and non-official worship practices?

Finally, as stated in my Introduction, the primary model of "official liturgy" that was held up throughout my study was the eucharistic liturgy, particularly the Sunday Eucharist as it was celebrated by one worshiping community and interpreted by eight ethnographic participants. Within the documents of Vatican II, the term "the liturgy" as source and summit, as it was first stated in article 10 of SC, eventually focused exclusively on the eucharistic liturgy (e.g., in article 11 of LG and article 5 of PO). This was not only indicative of what transpired throughout the course of the liturgical movement but also influenced subsequent official writings (e.g., the *Catechism of the Catholic Church* and the writings of Popes John Paul II and Benedict XVI). But what if we were to return to the term "the liturgy," before "The *Eucharist* as source and summit" became a popular mantra, and further investigate the interrelationship between other forms of *official* worship practices especially the Liturgy of the Hours) and non-official worship practices? Jude's use of the iPad during her recitation of the Office provided only one example. Further investigation in this area would not detract from my argument that "the liturgy of life" still serves as a better metaphor, particularly if we consider the dynamic interplay among all forms of worship practices and the maintenance of divine initiative in theological reflection. It would present a more structured network of official worship practices to consider in relationship to our everyday worship, and perhaps lessen any narrowing of "official liturgy" to eucharistic liturgy. In turn, pastoral leaders and worshiping communities would increasingly need to

---

[22] Katharine E. Harmon, *There Were Also Many Women There: Lay Women in the Liturgical Movement in the United States, 1926–59* (Collegeville, MN: Liturgical Press, 2013), 244.

consider what transpires beyond Sunday gatherings by better promoting other forms of official worship practices, such as communal or individual praying of morning and evening prayer.

At the same time, we must be attentive to new and developing concerns with regard to the ever-expanding contextual horizon of worship practices. In more recent times an emerging subfield within the sociology of religion has been the focus on "religion, media and culture."[23] Tracing back the roots of this subfield to the 1950s and 1960s, when concern over the relationship between "the media and cultures of everyday life" emerged in sociology, scholars find affinity with the work of sociologists of lived religion:

> The literature on religion, media and culture also shares common interests and concerns with the closely related work that has developed during the same period on "lived religion." . . . Both bodies of work are interested in everyday social and cultural practice, distinguishing themselves from approaches to the study of religion which focus on abstracted textual or doctrinal content, the practices and beliefs of religious elites, or broad macro-level generalizations about religion and society based on quantitative data on religious belief, identification and behavior. By contrast, researchers studying religion, media and culture and lived religion are often engaged in a common task of trying to understand how religious life worlds are lived out in the context of media-saturated, late capitalist societies.[24]

I already touched upon some of the implications of the use of electronic devices (the iPad and iPhone) in the interrelationship dynamics between worship practices. My concern is that liturgical theologians may ignore the very likelihood that such forms of

[23] See Eric Michael Mazur and Kate McCarthy, eds., *God in the Details: American Religion in Popular Culture*, 2d ed. (New York: Routledge, 2011); Gordon Lynch, Jolyon Mitchell, and Anna Strhan, eds., *Religion, Media and Culture: A Reader* (New York: Routledge, 2012); Daniel A. Stout, *Media and Religion: Foundations of an Emerging Field* (New York: Routledge, 2012); Rachel Wagner, *Godwired: Religion, Ritual, and Virtual Reality* (New York: Routledge, 2012).

[24] Lynch, Mitchell, and Strhan, *Religion, Media and Culture*, 2.

practice will increase among Christian worshipers and that the acceleration rate of advancing technologies may, in the end, outpace the development of historical and theological considerations.[25]

[25] Interest in this area is evident in the more recent contributions by Teresa Berger et al. in *Liturgy in Migration: From the Upper Room to Cyberspace*, ed. Teresa Berger (Collegeville, MN: Liturgical Press, 2012).

Conclusion

"We pray to Mary . . . but we *really* pray to God." The words of my religious education teacher, Mrs. Brunori, continue to echo in my memories of growing up Roman Catholic. In those days, if one were to ask me "who or what is the source and summit of your life?" I might have answered: "Invisible Mary." Today my reply would be more complex. In many ways this book serves as an academic extension of past attempts to interrelate the devotional practices of my childhood with the theological understandings I have learned as an adult, closely paralleling my journey from being a non-expert in theological disciplines to becoming someone who might be considered an expert. In my drive to comprehend and articulate these experiences I set out to examine the dynamic interrelationship between Sunday Eucharist and many forms of worship practice that mark the everyday lives of engaged Christians.

I framed my investigation within successive chapters encompassing theological, sociological, and ethnographic disciplines. My methodological approach demonstrates how theological-liturgical writings and social-scientific tools may perhaps be brought into dialogue with one another and, consequently, demonstrates how such correlations lead to new paradigms and metaphors for marking the interrelationships of Christian worship practices. Liturgical scholars may well benefit from this approach in two ways: this book (1) serves as an interdisciplinary model for liturgical studies by advancing how official statements, historical data, and theological/theoretical reflections could benefit from the fields of sociology and ethnography, and (2) it models a way of examining the interrelationship between official liturgy and practices of everyday worship that have existed in the past and have yet to be revealed, given the ever-expanding contextual horizon of worship practices.

What is perhaps most distinctive about this book is that I chose not to limit my resources to official, historical, and theological disciplines, but to extend my investigation to include the actual voices, experiences, and practices of non-experts. In order to facilitate this, I turned to sociological disciplines and borrowed ethnographic tools from Mary McGann, James Clifford, and a host of sociologists of lived religion. I expanded past cultural assumptions in the field of liturgical studies by bringing to light the non-official worship practices of everyday life and the accompanying interpretations that would otherwise have gone unnoticed. The interpretive data I gleamed from my fieldwork critiqued past approaches for understanding the interrelationship between official and non-official worship practices and led to new paradigms for understanding these relationships. As a result, the correlations I performed throughout the book expanded the contextual horizon of liturgical scholarship, while addressing a present theological concern that seeks to maintain the divine initiative.

As we peer into the future we note that the horizon of liturgical-theological inquiry continues to unfold before us, particularly since new or retrieved forms of worship practices have yet to be revealed. How these come to be interrelated with official liturgies is yet to be seen, but for now we may hold true to the conviction that God remains the source and summit of all these activities.

The 10:30 AM Sunday Eucharist of St. Agnes Church

Easter Season: A View from the Choir Loft

Fr. Raymond Allender, SJ

Front of St. Agnes Church on Masonic Avenue, San Francisco, California.

Members of the Choir

Mr. Franck Uranich, Director of Music and Liturgy

The Music Ministers with Schola Leading as Cantor

Appendix Two

The Hospitality Area of St. Agnes Church

Appendix Three

Helen Rosario's Home

Bedroom Altar in front of Bed

Bedroom Altar behind the Bed

"Third Altar"
in Hallway

Papal Blessing

Helen's Two Prayer Journals

Dining Room Altar

Appendix Four

The Everyday Prayer Schedule of Helen Rosario

7:00 AM   Helen wakes up and "thanks God": "I reached another morning. I have to thank God that I'm still alive. I stay in my bed because I have my altar in front of me."

Sitting on top of the side table next to her bed are two very old "prayer books." Originally these books contained blank pages, but over the years (she doesn't remember how long ago this began), Helen pasted, taped, and wrote a variety of prayers and inserted pictures of saints. She has memorized most of these prayers and their sequence is dependent on her intentions for that day,

7:00 AM to 4 PM   Every hour, on the hour, she recites the novena to the Infant of Prague.[1] For the past several months she

[1] Prayer Text: O Jesus, Who has said, "Ask and you shall receive, seek and you shall find, knock and it shall be opened," through the intercession of Mary, Your Most Holy Mother, I knock, I seek, I ask that my prayer be granted. (*Make your request.*) O Jesus, Who has said, "All that you ask of the Father in My Name, He will grant you," through the intercession of Mary Your Most Holy Mother, I humbly and urgently ask your Father in your name that my prayer will be granted. (*Make your request.*) O Jesus, Who has said, "Heaven and earth shall pass away but My word shall not pass away," through the intercession of Mary Your Most Holy Mother, I feel confident that my prayer will be granted. (*Make your request.*)
Prayer of Thanksgiving: Divine Infant Jesus, I know You love me and would never leave me. I thank You for Your close Presence in my life. Miraculous

has been focusing on her granddaughter, a high school student who "needs help in studying."

8:30 AM   After breakfast, Helen leaves the house for daily Mass at St. Agnes.

12:00 PM   Helen recites "her favorite prayer" of the day, the Angelus Prayer.[2]

6:00 PM   Second recitation of the Angelus Prayer.

8:00 PM and 11 PM   After watching *Jeopardy/Wheel of Fortune*, Helen recites another set of prayers, beginning at 8:00 PM and continuing before she retires to bed around 11:00 PM. These include, but are not limited to: the rosary (using the assigned mysteries of the day), and, more recently, prayers to St. Anthony, St. Jude, and St. Fina.

Infant, I believe in Your promise of peace, blessings, and freedom from want. I place every need and care in Your hands. Lord Jesus, may I always trust in Your generous mercy and love. I want to honor and praise You, now and forever. Amen.

[2] Prayer Text: The Angel of the Lord declared unto Mary: And she conceived of the Holy Spirit. Hail Mary, full of grace, the Lord is with thee; blessed art thou among women and blessed is the fruit of thy womb, Jesus. Holy Mary, Mother of God, pray for us sinners, now and at the hour of our death. Amen.

Behold the handmaid of the Lord: Be it done unto me according to Thy word. Hail Mary . . .

And the Word was made Flesh and dwelt among us. Hail Mary . . .

Pray for us, O Holy Mother of God, that we may be made worthy of the promises of Christ.

Let us pray: Pour forth, we beseech Thee, O Lord, Thy grace into our hearts; that we, to whom the incarnation of Christ, Thy Son, was made known by the message of an angel, may by His Passion and Cross be brought to the glory of His Resurrection, through the same Christ Our Lord. Amen.

"This Is Church!"

Photos by Irene Duller

Upon learning of one of Irene's everyday worship practices, I invited her to take photos of these experiences with her cell phone. The descriptions and titles are her own.

Chicago Sky — "Alleluia Sky"
March 22, 2012

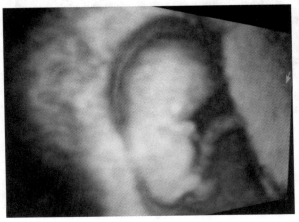

"Finding out we're pregnant!"
January 6, 2012

Planting at Home — "Offering"
March 25, 2012

Chicago Street Art — "Homily"
March 21, 2012

Bibliography

Official Documents

Benedict XVI. Post-Synodal Apostolic Exhortation, *Sacramentum Caritatis*. Washington, DC: United States Catholic Conference, 2007.

Catechism of the Catholic Church. Promulgated by Pope John Paul II. Vatican City: Libreria Editrice Vaticana, 1997.

Catechism of the Council of Trent. Promulgated by Pope Pius V (1566). Translated by Theodore Alois Buckley. London: George Routledge and Company, 1852.

Congregation for Divine Worship and the Discipline of the Sacraments. *Directory on Popular Piety and the Liturgy: Principles and Guidelines.* Vatican City: Libreria Editrice Vaticana, 2001.

Constitution on the Sacred Liturgy. Promulgated by Pope Paul VI (December 4, 1963). In *The Liturgy Documents: A Parish Resource*, 1–30. Vol. 1. 4th ed. Chicago: Liturgy Training Publications, 2004.

Decree on the Ministry and Life of Priests. In *Vatican Council II: The Basic Sixteen Documents*, edited by Austin Flannery, 317–64. Rev. ed. Collegeville, MN: Liturgical Press, 2014.

Dogmatic Constitution on the Church. In *Vatican Council II: The Basic Sixteen Documents*, edited by Austin Flannery, 1–95. Rev. ed. Collegeville, MN: Liturgical Press, 2014.

John Paul II. An Apostolic Letter Issued "Motu Proprio" *The Lord's Day.* Washington, DC: United States Catholic Conference, 1998.

Leo XIII. Encyclical Letter *Mirae Caritatis* (1902): http://www.vatican.va /holy_father/leo_xiii/encyclicals/documents/hf_l-xiii_enc_28051902 _mirae-caritatis_en.html.

Nairobi Statement on Worship and Culture: Contemporary Challenges and Opportunities. Lutheran World Federation's Study Team on Worship and Culture. Nairobi, Kenya, Third International Consultation, 1996. In

187

Christian Worship Worldwide: Expanding Horizons, Deepening Practices, edited by Charles E. Farhadian, 285–90. Grand Rapids, MI: William B. Eerdmans Publishing Company, 2007.

Pius X. An Apostolic Letter Issued "Motu Proprio," *Tra Le Sollecitudini, ASS* 36 (November 22, 1903). In *The New Liturgy: A Documentation, 1903–1965,* edited by R. Kevin Seasoltz, 3–10. New York: Herder and Herder, 1966.

———. Decree of the Sacred Congregation of the Council, *Sacra Tridentina Synodus, ASS* 38 (December 22, 1905). In *The New Liturgy: A Documentation, 1903–1965,* edited by R. Kevin Seasoltz, 11–15. New York: Herder and Herder, 1966.

Pius XII. Encyclical Letter, *Mystici Corporis Christi, AAS* 35 (June 29, 1943). In *The New Liturgy: A Documentation, 1903-1965,* edited by R. Kevin Seasoltz, 64–102. New York: Herder and Herder, 1966.

———. Encyclical Letter, *Mediator Dei, AAS* 39 (November 20, 1947). In *The New Liturgy: A Documentation, 1903-1965,* edited by R. Kevin Seasoltz, 107–59. New York: Herder and Herder, 1966.

Other Sources

Adam, Adolf. *The Eucharistic Celebration: The Source and Summit of Faith.* Translated by Robert C. Schultz. Collegeville, MN: Liturgical Press, 1994.

Albert-Llorca, Marlène. "Renouveau de la religion locale." In *Identitiés religieuses en Europe,* edited by Grace Davie and Danièle Hervieu-Léger, 235–52. Paris: La Découverte, 1996.

Ammerman, Nancy T. *Bible Believers: Fundamentalists in the Modern World.* New Brunswick, NJ: Rutgers University Press, 1987.

———, ed. *Everyday Religion: Observing Modern Religious Lives.* Oxford: Oxford University Press, 2007.

———. "Religious Identities and Religious Institutions." In *Handbook of Sociology of Religion,* edited by Michele Dillon, 207–24. Cambridge, UK: Cambridge University Press, 2003.

Ammerman, Nancy T., Jackson W. Carroll, Carl S. Dudley, and William McKinney, eds. *Studying Congregations: A New Handbook.* Nashville, TN: Abingdon Press, 1998.

Arbuckle, Gerald A. *Culture, Inculturation, and Theologians: A Postmodern Critique.* Collegeville, MN: Liturgical Press, 2010.

Asad, Talal. "Anthropological Conceptions of Religion: Reflections on Geertz." *Man* 18 (1983): 237–59.

———. *Genealogies of Religion: Discipline and Reasons for Power in Christianity and Islam.* Baltimore: John Hopkins University Press, 1993.

Aune, Michael B. "Liturgy and Theology: Rethinking the Relationship." *Worship* 81 (2007): 46–68, 141–69.

Barbour, Ian. *Religion in an Age of Science.* New York: Harper & Row, 1979.

Barnard, Alan. *History and Theory in Anthropology.* Cambridge, UK: Cambridge University Press, 2000.

Barthes, Roland. *Mythologies.* Translated by Annette Lavers. New York: Hill and Wang, 1972.

Bartkowski, John P. "Connections and Contradictions: Exploring the Complex Linkages between Faith and Family." In *Everyday Religion: Observing Modern Religious Lives*, edited by Nancy T. Ammerman, 153–66. Oxford: Oxford University Press, 2007.

Beauduin, Dom Lambert. "La Vraie Prière de L'Église: Rapport présenté par le R.P. Dom Lambert Beaudoin (sic) O.S.B." *Questions Liturgiques* 91 (2010): 37–41.

Beauduin, Lambert. *Liturgy: the Life of Church (Le piété de l'église: principes et faits).* Translated by Virgil Michel. Collegeville, MN: Liturgical Press, 1926.

Bell, Catherine. *Ritual Theory, Ritual Practice.* New York: Oxford University Press, 1992.

———. *Ritual: Perspectives and Dimensions.* New York: Oxford, 1997.

Bender, Courtney. *Heaven's Kitchen: Living Religion at God's Love We Deliver.* Chicago: University of Chicago Press, 2003.

Berger, Teresa, et al. *Liturgy in Migration: From the Upper Room to Cyberspace,* ed. Teresa Berger. Collegeville, MN: Liturgical Press, 2012.

Biernacki, Richard. "Method and Metaphor after the New Cultural History." In *Beyond the Cultural Turn: New Directions in the Study of Society and Culture,* edited by Victoria E. Bonnell and Lynn Hunt, 62–92. Berkeley: University of California Press, 1999.

Bonnell, Victoria E., and Lynn Hunt, eds. *Beyond the Cultural Turn.* Berkeley: University of California Press, 1999.

Botte, Bernard. *From Silence to Participation: An Insider's View of Liturgical Renewal.* Translated by John Sullivan. Washington, DC: Pastoral Press, 1988.

Bourdieu, Pierre. *Distinction: A Social Critique of the Judgment of Taste*. Translated by Richard Nice. Cambridge, MA: Harvard University Press, 1984.

———. *Esquisse d'une theorie de la pratique. Precede de trois etudes d'ethnologie kabyle*. Cambridge, UK: Cambridge University Press, 1972.

Bradshaw, Paul F. "Difficulties in Doing Liturgical Theology." *Pacifica* 11 (1998): 181–94.

———. *The Search for the Origins of Christian Worship*. 2nd ed. Oxford: Oxford University Press, 2002.

Bugnini, Annibale. *The Reform of the Liturgy: 1948–1975*. Collegeville, MN: Liturgical Press, 1990.

Casel, Odo. *The Mystery of Christian Worship*. Westminster, MD: The Newman Press, 1962.

Chaves, Mark. *Congregations in America*. Cambridge, MA: Harvard University Press, 2004.

Chupungco, Anscar J. "Inculturation of Worship: Forty Years of Progress and Tradition." Paper 5. Valparaiso, IN: The Liturgical Institute Conference Proceedings, 2003.

———. *Liturgical Inculturation: Sacramentals, Religiosity, and Catechesis*. Collegeville, MN: Liturgical Press, 1992.

———. "Liturgy and Inculturation." In *Handbook for Liturgical Studies*, edited by Anscar J. Chupungco, vol. 2, 337–75. Collegeville, MN: Liturgical Press, 1998.

———. *What, Then, Is Liturgy? Musings and Memoir*. Collegeville, MN: Liturgical Press, 2010.

Clifford, James. *Routes: Travel and Translation in the Late Twentieth Century*. Cambridge, MA: Harvard University Press, 1997.

Clifford, James, and George E. Marcus, eds. *Writing Culture: The Poetics and Politics of Ethnography*. Berkeley: The University of California Press, 1986.

Collins, Mary. "An Adventuresome Hypothesis: Women as Authors of Liturgical Change." Response to the Berakah Award. In *Proceedings of the North American Academy of Liturgy* (1993).

———. "Liturgical Methodology and the Cultural Evolution of Worship in the United States." *Worship* 49 (1975): 85–102.

———. "Ritual Symbols and the Ritual Process: The Work of Victor W. Turner." *Worship* 50 (1976): 336–46.

———. *Worship: Renewal to Practice*. Washington, DC: Pastoral Press, 1987.

Collins, Randall. "The Classical Tradition in Sociology of Religion." In *The Sage Handbook of the Sociology of Religion*, edited by James A. Beckford and N. J. Demerath III, 19–38. London: Sage Publication, 2007.

———. *Interaction Ritual Chains*. Princeton, NJ: Princeton University Press, 2004.

Crapanzano, Vincent. "Hermes' Dilemma." In *Writing Culture: The Poetics and Politics of Ethnography*, edited by James Clifford and George E. Marcus, 68–76. Berkeley: The University of California Press, 1986.

Crowley, Eileen D. *Liturgical Art for a Media Culture*. Collegeville, MN: Liturgical Press, 2007.

Davie, Grace. "The Evolution of the Sociology of Religion: Theme and Variation." In *The Handbook of the Sociology of Religion*, edited by Michele Dillon, 61–75. Cambridge, UK: Cambridge University Press, 2003.

De Certeau, Michel. *The Practice of Everyday Life*. Translated by Steven Rendall. Berkeley: The University of California Press, 1984.

Derrida, Jacque. *Of Grammatology*. Translated by Gayatri Chakravorty Spivak. Baltimore: Johns Hopkins University Press, 1976.

Diaz-Salazar, Rafael. *El capital simbolico: Estrcutura social, politica y religion en España*. Madrid: HOAC, 1988.

Dillon, Michele. *In the Course of a Lifetime*. Berkeley: The University of California Press, 2007.

———. *Catholic Identity: Balancing Reason, Faith, and Power*. Cambridge, UK: Cambridge University Press, 1999.

Douglas, Mary. *Natural Symbols: Explorations in Cosmology*. New York: Pantheon Books, 1982.

Driscoll, Jeremy. "Worship in the Spirit of Logos: Romans 12:1-2 and the Source and Summit of Christian Life." *Letter & Spirit* 5 (2009): 77–101.

Durkheim, Émile. *The Elementary Forms of Religious Life*. Translated by Karen E. Fields. New York: The Free Press, 1995.

Egan, Harvey D. "The Mysticism of Everyday Life." *Studies in Formative Spirituality* 10 (1989): 7–26.

Elias, Norbert. "On the Concept of Everyday Life." In *The Norbert Elias Reader: A Biographical Selection*, edited by Johan Goudsbloom and Stephen Mennel, 166–74. Oxford: Blackwell Publishers, Ltd., 1998.

Empereur, James. "Popular Piety and the Liturgy: Principles and Guidelines." In *Directory on Popular Piety and the Liturgy: Principles and Guidelines;*

A Commentary, edited by Peter C. Phan, 1–17. Collegeville, MN: Liturgical Press, 2005.

Ewick, Patricia, and Susan S. Silbey. *The Common Place of Law.* Chicago, IL: The University of Chicago Press, 1998.

Fagerberg, David. *Theologia Prima: What Is Liturgical Theology?* Collegeville, MN: Liturgical Press, 1992.

Farhadian, Charles E., ed. *Christian Worship Worldwide: Expanding Horizons, Deepening Practices.* Grand Rapids, MI: William B. Eerdmans Publishing Company, 2007.

Flanagan, Kiernan. *Sociology and Liturgy: Re-presentations of the Holy.* New York: St. Martin's Press, 1991.

Ferrone, Rita. *Liturgy:* Sacrosanctum Concilium. Mahwah, NJ: Paulist Press, 2007.

Foley, Edward. *From Age to Age: How Christians Have Celebrated the Eucharist.* Rev. and exp. ed. Chicago: Liturgy Training Publications, 2008.

Foucault, Michel. *The Archaeology of Knowledge and the Discourse on Language.* Translated by A. M. Sheridan Smith. New York: Pantheon Books. 1972.

———. *Discipline and Punish: The Birth of the Prison.* Translated by Alan Sheridan. New York: Vintage Books, 1977.

———. *The Order of Things: An Archaeology of the Human Sciences.* New York: Vintage Books, 1970.

Francis, Mark R. *Local Worship, Global Church: Popular Religion and the Liturgy.* Collegeville, MN: Liturgical Press, 2014.

———. "Liturgy and Popular Piety in a Historical Perspective." In *Directory on Popular Piety and the Liturgy: Principles and Guidelines; A Commentary,* edited by Peter C. Phan, 39–42. Collegeville, MN: Liturgical Press, 2005.

Froechlé-Chopard, Marie Helène. "Les Dévotions populaires d'après les visites pastorals: Un Example: le Diocèse de Vence au début du XVIIIe siècle." *Revue d'histoire de l'église de France* 60 (1974): 85–86.

Funk, Virgil. "The Liturgical Movement (1830–1969)." In *The New Dictionary of Sacramental Theology,* edited by Peter E. Fink, 695–715. Collegeville, MN: Liturgical Press, 1990.

Geertz, Clifford. *The Interpretation of Cultures.* New York: Basic Books, 1973.

Ghosh, Amitav. "The Imam and the Indian." *Granta* 20 (Winter 1986): 135–46.

Giner, Salvador, and Salvador Sarasa, eds. *Religión y sociedad en España.* Madrid: CIS, 1993.

Giordan, Giuseppe, and William H. Swatos Jr., eds. *Religion, Spirituality and Everyday Practices*. New York/Heidelberg, Germany: Springer, 2011.

Goffman, Erving. *The Presentation of Self in Everyday Life*. New York: Anchor Books, 1959.

Greenblatt, Stephen. "The Touch of the Real." In *The Fate of "Culture": Geertz and Beyond*, edited by Sherry B. Ortner, 14–29. Berkeley: The University of California Press, 1999.

Grillmeier, Aloys. "The People of God." In *Commentary on the Documents of Vatican II*, vol. 1, edited by Herbert Vorgrimler, 156–85. New York: Herder and Herder, 1967.

Grimes, Ronald L. *Beginnings in Ritual Studies*. Rev. ed. Columbia: University of South Carolina Press, 1995.

———. *Rite out of Place: Ritual, Media, and the Arts*. Oxford: Oxford University Press, 2006.

Gueranger, Prosper. *Institute liturgiques*. Paris: Société Génerale de Librairie Catholique, 1878.

———. *L'Année Liturgique. Librairie Religieuse H. Oudin*. Paris, 1909.

Hall, David D., ed. *Lived Religion in America: Toward a History of Practice*. Princeton, NJ: Princeton University Press, 1997.

Haquin, André. "Dom L. Beauduin et le Congrès des Oeuvres Catholiques de Malines: A l'occasion du centenaire du Mouvement liturgique belge (1909–2009)." *Questiones Liturgiques* 91 (2010): 18–36.

———. "The Liturgical Movement and Catholic Ritual Revision." In *The Oxford History of Christian Worship*, edited by Geoffrey Wainwright and Karen B. Westerfield Tucker, 696–720. Cambridge, UK: Cambridge University Press, 2006.

Harmon, Katherine E. *There Were Also Many Women There: Lay Women in the Liturgical Movement in the United States, 1926–59*. Collegeville, MN: Liturgical Press, 2013.

Highmore, Ben. *Everyday Life and Cultural Theory: An Introduction*. New York: Routledge, 2002.

———. "Introduction: Questioning Everyday Life." In *The Everyday Life Reader*, edited by Ben Highmore, 1–34. New York: Routledge, 2002.

Hoffman, Lawrence A. *Beyond the Text: A Holistic Approach to Liturgy*. Bloomington: Indiana University Press, 1987.

Holtmann, Cathy. "Workers in the Vineyard: Catholic Women and Social Action." In *Religion, Spirituality and Everyday Practices*, edited by Giuseppe Giordan and William H. Swatos Jr., 141–52. New York/ Heidelberg, Germany: Springer, 2011.

Hunt, Stephen. *Religion and Everyday Life*. London: Routledge, 2005.

Irwin, Kevin. "*Lex Orandi, Lex Credendi*—Origins and Meaning: State of the Question." *Liturgical Ministry* 11 (Spring 2002): 57–69.

———. "A Spirited Community Encounters Christ: Liturgical and Sacramental Theology and Practice." In *Catholic Theology Facing the Future: Historical Perspectives*, edited by Dermot A. Lane, 95–122. Mahwah, NJ: Paulist Press, 2003.

Johnson, Cuthbert. *Prosper Guéranger (1805–1875): A Liturgical Theologian*. Rome: The Pontifical Institute of St. Anselm, 1984.

Jungmann, Josef Andreas. "Constitution on the Sacred Liturgy." In *Commentary on the Documents of Vatican II*, edited by Herbert Vorgrimler, vol. 1, 1–87. New York: Herder and Herder, 1967.

Kavanagh, Aidan. *On Liturgical Theology*. New York: Pueblo, 1984.

Kelleher, Margaret Mary. "The Communion Rite: A Study of Roman Catholic Liturgical Performance." *Journal of Ritual Studies* 5, no. 2 (Summer 1991): 99–122.

Lan, Kwok Pui. "Empire and the Study of Religion." Presidential address, annual meeting of the American Academy of Religion, San Francisco, CA, November 19, 2011.

Lathrop, Gordon. *Holy Things: A Liturgical Theology*. Minneapolis, MN: Fortress Press, 1993.

Lawn, Brian. *The Rise and Decline of the Scholastic Questio Disputata*. Leiden: E. J. Brill, 1993.

Lefebvre, Henri. *Critique of Everyday Life*. Translated by John Moore. London: Verso, 1991.

Lynch, Gordon, Jolyon Mitchell, and Anna Strhan, eds. *Religion, Media and Culture: A Reader*, New York: Routledge, 2012.

Marshall, Paul V. "Reconsidering 'Liturgical Theology': Is There a *Lex Orandi* for All Christians?" *Studia Liturgica* 25 (1995): 129–50.

Mazur, Eric Michael, and Kate McCarthy, eds. *God in the Details: American Religion in Popular Culture*. 2nd ed. New York: Routledge, 2011.

McGann, Mary E. *A Precious Fountain: Music in the Worship of an African American Catholic Community*. Collegeville, MN: Liturgical Press, 2004.

———. *Exploring Music as Worship and Theology: Research in Liturgical Practice*. Collegeville, MN: Liturgical Press, 2002.

McGuire, Meredith B. "Contested Meaning and Definitional Boundaries: Historicizing the Sociology of Religion." In *Defining Religion*. Vol. 10: *Investigating the Boundaries Between Sacred and Secular*, edited by Arthur L. Greil and David G. Bromley, 127–38. Religion and the Social Order. Greenwich, CT: JAL, 2003.

———. "Embodied Practices: Negotiation and Resistance." In *Everyday Religion: Observing Modern Religious Lives*, edited by Nancy T. Ammerman, 187–200. Oxford: Oxford University Press, 2007.

———. *Lived Religion: Faith and Practice in Everyday Life*. Oxford: Oxford University Press, 2008.

———. *Religion: The Social Context*. 5th ed. New York: Wadsworth Group, 2002.

Michel, Patrick. *Politique et Religion: La Grande Mutation*. Paris: Albin Michel, 1996.

Michel, Virgil. *Our Life in Christ*. Collegeville, MN: Liturgical Press, 1939.

Mitchell, Nathan. *Liturgy and the Social Sciences*. Collegeville, MN: Liturgical Press, 1999.

Muir, Edward. *Ritual in Early Modern Europe*. 2nd ed. Cambridge, UK: Cambridge University Press, 2005.

Neitz, Mary Jo. "Lived Religion: Signposts of Where We Have Been and Where We Can Go from Here." In *Religion, Spirituality and Everyday Practices*, edited by Giuseppe Giordan and William H. Swatos Jr., 45–56. New York/Heidelberg, Germany: Springer, 2011.

O'Connor, James T. "The Eucharist: Source and Summit of Justice and Charity." *Social Justice Review* 81 (Nov.–Dec. 1990): 197–99.

Orsi, Robert A. *The Madonna of 115th Street: Faith and Community in Italian Harlem, 1880–1950*. New Haven, CT: Yale University Press, 1985, 2002.

Ortner, Sherry. "Theory in Anthropology Since the Sixties." *Comparative Studies in Society and History* 26 (1984): 144–57.

Pace, Enzo. "Religion as Communication: The Changing Shape of Catholicism in Europe." In *Everyday Religion: Observing Modern Religious Lives*, edited by Nancy T. Ammerman, 37–49. Oxford: Oxford University Press, 2007.

Pecklers, Keith F. *The Unread Vision: The Liturgical Movement in the United States of America: 1926–1955.* Collegeville, MN: Liturgical Press, 1998.

———. "Vatican II and the Liturgical Renewal: An Unfinished Agenda." *East Asian Pastoral Review* 42 (2005): 26.

Pfatteicher, Philip. "Worship: The Source and Summit of Faith." *Consensus* 9, no. 2 (1983): 13–25.

Phan, Peter C. *Being Religious Interreligiously: Asian Perspectives on Interfaith Dialogue in Postmodernity.* Maryknoll, NY: Orbis Books, 2004.

———, ed. *Directory on Popular Piety and the Liturgy: Principles and Guidelines; A Commentary.* Collegeville, MN: Liturgical Press, 2005.

———. "Liturgy of Life as the 'Summit and Source' of the Eucharistic Liturgy: Church Worship as Symbolization of the Liturgy of Life?" In *Incongruities: Who We Are and How We Pray,* edited by Timothy Fitzgerald and David A. Lysik, 5–33. Chicago: Liturgy Training Publications, 2000.

Pierce, Joanne M., and Michael Downey, eds. *Source and Summit: Commemorating Josef A. Jungman, S.J.* Collegeville, MN: Liturgical Press, 1999.

Quitslund, Sonya. *Beauduin: A Prophet Vindicated.* New York: Newman Press, 1973.

Rahner, Karl. "Considerations on the Active Role of the Person in the Sacramental Event." *Theological Investigations* 14. Translated by David Bourke, 161–65. New York: Seabury Press, 1976.

———. "Experience of the Holy Spirit." *Theological Investigations* 18. Translated by Edward Quinn, 189–97. New York: Crossroad, 1981.

———. "On the Theology of Worship." *Theological Investigations* 19. Translated by Edward Quinn, 141–49. New York: Crossroad, 1983.

———. "Reflections on the Experience of Grace." *Theological Investigations,* 3. Translated by Karl-H Kruger and Boniface Kruger, 86–90. New York: Crossroad, 1982.

———. *Spirit in the World.* Translated by William Dych. New York: Herder and Herder, 1968,

———. "The Theology of the Symbol." *Theological Investigations,* 4. Translated by Kevin Smyth, 221–52. Baltimore: Helicon, 1966.

Reid, Alcuin. *The Organic Development of the Liturgy: The Principles of Liturgical Reform and Their Relation to the Twentieth-Century Liturgical Movement*

Prior to the Second Vatican Council. St. Michael's Abbey Press, Farnborough, England, 2004.

Roof, Wade Clark. "Religion and Spirituality: Toward an Integrated Analysis." In *The Handbook of the Sociology of Religion,* edited by Michele Dillon, 137–50. Cambridge, UK: Cambridge University Press, 2003.

Sahlins, Marshal. *Culture and Practical Reason.* Chicago: University of Chicago Press, 1976.

Sartore, Domenico. "Le manifestazione della religiosità." *Anamnesis* 7 (Genoa, 1989): 232–33.

Schmemann, Alexander. *Introduction to Liturgical Theology.* London: The Faith Press, 1966.

Schneider, Mark A. *Culture and Enchantment.* Chicago: University of Chicago Press, 1993.

Schreiter, Robert J. *Constructing Local Theologies.* Maryknoll, NY: Orbis Books.

Schilson, Arno. "Liturgy as 'Summit and Source' of Christian Life: Origin and Meaning of a Programmatic Conciliar Phrase." *Living Light* 31 (Spring 1995): 57–67.

Searle, Mark. "The Notre Dame Study of Catholic Parish Life." *Worship* 60, no. 4 (1986): 312–33.

Senn, Frank C. *The People's Work: A Social History of the Liturgy.* Minneapolis, MN: Fortress Press, 2006.

Sewell, William H. *Logics of History: Social Theory and Social Transformation.* Chicago: University of Chicago Press, 2005.

Shankman, Paul. "The Thick and the Thin: On the Interpretive Theoretical Program of Clifford Geertz." *Current Anthropology* 25, no. 3 (1984): 261–79.

Skelley, Michael. *The Liturgy of the World: Karl Rahner's Theology of Worship.* Collegeville, MN: Liturgical Press, 1991.

———. "Modern Theologians and Liturgical Renewal." In *The New Dictionary of Sacramental Worship,* edited by Peter E. Fink, 1245–58. Collegeville, MN: Liturgical Press, 1990.

Spillman, Lyn, ed. *Cultural Sociology.* Malden, MA: Blackwell Publishers, 2002.

Stout, Daniel A. *Media and Religion: Foundations of an Emerging Field.* New York: Routledge, 2012.

197

Stringer, Martin D. *A Sociological History of Christian Worship.* Cambridge, UK: Cambridge University Press, 2005.

Swatos, William H., and Giuseppe Giordan. "The Spiritual 'Turn' in Religion as Process and Outcome." In *Religion, Spirituality and Everyday Practices,* edited by Giuseppe Giordan and William H. Swatos Jr., x–xv. New York/Heidelberg, Germany: Springer, 2011.

Swidler, Ann. "Culture in Action: Symbols and Strategies." *American Sociological Review* 51, no. 2 (April 1986): 273–86.

———. *Talk of Love: How Culture Matters.* Chicago: University of Chicago Press, 2001.

Taft, Robert. "Response to the Berakah Award: Anamnesis." *Worship* 59 (1985): 305–25.

Tanner, Kathryn. *Theories of Culture: A New Agenda for Theology.* Cambridge, UK: Cambridge University Press, 1997.

Turner, Victor. *Dramas, Fields and Metaphors.* Ithaca, NY: Cornell University Press, 1974.

———. *The Forest of Symbols: Aspects of Ndembu Ritual.* Ithaca, NY: Cornell University Press, 1967.

———. *The Ritual Process: Structure and Anti-Structure.* Chicago: Aldine, 1969.

Vogel, Dwight W. "Liturgical Theology: A Conceptual Geography." In *Primary Sources of Liturgical Theology: A Reader*, edited by Dwight W. Vogel, 3–14. Collegeville, MN: Liturgical Press, 2000.

Wagner, Rachel. *Godwired: Religion, Ritual, and Virtual Reality.* New York: Routledge, 2012.

Weber, Max. *The Protestant Ethic and the Spirit of Capitalism.* New York: Scribner, 1958.

———. *The Sociology of Religion.* Translated by Ephraim Fischoff. Boston, MA: Beacon Press, 1963.

Williams, Raymond. *Marxism and Literature.* Oxford: Oxford University Press, 1977.

White, James. *Roman Catholic Worship: Trent to Today.* Collegeville, MN: Liturgical Press, 2003.

Woodhead, Linda. "Spirituality and Christianity: The Unfolding of a Tangled Relationship." In *Religion, Spirituality and Everyday Practices*, edited by Giuseppe Giordan and William H. Swatos Jr., 3–21. New York/Heidelberg, Germany: Springer, 2011.

Wuthnow, Robert. *After Heaven: Spirituality in America Since the 1950s.* Princeton, NJ: Princeton University Press, 1998.

———. *Producing the Sacred: An Essay on Public Religion.* Urbana: University of Illinois Press, 1994.

Subject Index

Index of Names